T0208971

MY BOOK OF
FAITH
Declaration

Speaking the Seed of God's Word for a Fruitful Life

DR. KEN EZIMOHA

WESTBOW
PRESS®
A DIVISION OF THOMAS NELSON
& ZONDERVAN

WestBow Press books may be ordered through booksellers or by contacting:

WestBow Press
A Division of Thomas Nelson & Zondervan
1663 Liberty Drive
Bloomington, IN 47403
www.westbowpress.com
844-714-3454

ISBN: 978-1-6642-3661-5 (sc)
ISBN: 978-1-6642-3663-9 (hc)
ISBN: 978-1-6642-3662-2 (e)

Library of Congress Control Number: 2021911472

Print information available on the last page.

WestBow Press rev. date: 07/19/2021

CONTENTS

DEDICATION

I dedicate this book first to God my Father, my Lord, and my Helper.
I also dedicate it to my wife Mary, our children Zion, Judah, Joy and
Lily, to our parents Christopher, Stella, Alice, and Michael.

INTRODUCTION

This book is designed as a practical manual for everyone who would love to speak more of God's Word over every area of their lives. The goal is that, through practically speaking the Word of God, you will see the Word produce results by transforming your life and situation. By consistently speaking the Word of God over your life, you are planting seeds of God's Word in your life and will surely experience the manifestation of a fruitful harvest of blessings. Your life is like a farmland—whatever seeds you plant are what you will harvest.

> You will also declare a thing, And it will be established for you; So light will shine on your ways. (Job 22:28 New King James Version, NKJV)

Get ready! A life full of testimonies is assured because God's Word always works and accomplishes what it says. God said in Isaiah 55:10–11 (God's Word Translation, GWT; emphasis added), "Rain and snow come down from the sky. They do not go back again until they water the earth. They make it sprout and grow so that it produces seed for farmers and food for people to eat. *My word, which comes from my mouth*, is like the rain and snow. *It will not come back to me without results. It will accomplish whatever I want and achieve whatever I send it to do."*

God's Word is producing results in your life as you speak it.

> For assuredly, I say to you, *whoever says* to this mountain, "Be removed and be cast into the sea," and does not doubt in his heart, but *believes* that those things he says will be done, *he will have whatever he says.* (Mark 11:23 NKJV, emphasis added)

In the Bible verse above, Jesus teaches that our declarations made in faith will be done for us and we will have what we say or declare. As you declare more of God's Word, you will grow in faith and sprout by making new progress. You will grow spiritually and in every other area of your life, producing fruits and enjoying a blessed life from glory to glory. You will experience the manifestation of the power of God's Word in your life.

The Bible says in Habakkuk 2:14 (New International Version, NIV), "For the earth will be filled with the knowledge of the glory of the Lord as the waters cover the sea." My joy is helping enrich the lives of people around the world with the knowledge of his will for our lives in faith and in practical experience.

WHAT IS A FAITH DECLARATION?

A declaration is a power-filled statement based on truth; the Word of God is truth. John 17:17 (NKJV) says, "Your word is truth." This power-filled statement of truth has the ability to produce what it talks about in the life of the speaker who believes.

Daily repetition of faith declarations is a commitment to specific results in our lives based on God's Word. It is our being intentional about applying the transforming power of God's Word to our lives and situations to produce the good life. God's Word is the good news that produces the good life.

A faith declaration is not a wish, a desire, or mere positive thinking. It is God's thoughts spoken in God's words.

Declaring faith is utilizing the creative power of God's Word. When you declare something, you create something. If you declare good things, you create good things. If you declare bad things, you create bad things. Proverbs 18:21 (New Living Translation, NLT) says, "The tongue can bring death or life; those who love to talk will reap the consequences." God created everything by declaring them into being. Genesis 1:3 (King

James Version, KJV) says, "And God said, Let there be light: and there was light.

Faith declaration is simply declaring our faith; faith comes by the Word. It is when we speak God's Word over our lives, when we speak what we believe from God's Word to ourselves, when we agree by saying what God has said concerning us, and when we confess God's Word to ourselves over and over again.

Faith declaration can be synonymous with *faith proclamation, faith confession*, or *faith profession*.

The Word of God clearly tells us to do this. It is not enough to believe God's Word. The Word must be *spoken.*

> It is written: "I believed; therefore I have spoken."
> Since we have that same spirit of faith, we also believe
> and therefore speak. (2 Corinthians 4:13 NIV)

God wants us to do well in every area of our lives because he loves us so much, just like every good parent loves his or her child to do well in every area of life. One of the reasons he gave us his Word is that through the active speaking of the Word, we can transform every area of our lives for good. Jesus clearly said in Mark 11:23 (NKJV),

> For assuredly, I say to you, whoever says to this
> mountain, "Be removed and be cast into the sea,"
> and does not doubt in his heart, but believes that
> those things he says will be done, he will have
> whatever he says.

God created the whole world with the words "Let there be" and "there was." In Genesis 1, he transformed the earth from a dark, formless, and empty mass to a beautiful earth with structure, life, plants, animals, and great views. By declaring our faith, we apply the creative power of God's Word to recreate our lives. You can redesign your life and future by the words you believe and speak over yourself today.

God Expects Us to Declare or Confess Our Faith

God expects us to believe, *speak,* and do his Word. Speaking the Word enables and causes us to do the Word.

The Bible says in Job 22:28 (NKJV), "You will also declare a thing, And it will be established for you; So light will shine on your ways."

In Joshua 1:8 (GWT), God himself tells Joshua, "Never stop reciting these teachings. You must think about them night and day so that you will faithfully do everything written in them. Only then will you prosper and succeed."

In 2 Corinthians 4:13 (NKJV), the Word says, "And since we have the same spirit of faith, according to what is written, 'I believed and therefore I spoke,' we also believe and therefore speak."

These scriptures make it clear to us that our faith should be a *spoken* declaration.

The Bible teaches that the things that are freely given to us by God have to be *spoken* with words that God teaches us. In 1 Corinthians 2:12–13 (NKJV), we read,

> Now we have received, not the spirit of the world, but the Spirit who is from God, that we might know the things that have been freely given to us by God. These things we also speak, not in words which man's wisdom teaches but which the Holy Spirit teaches, comparing spiritual things with spiritual.

We receive salvation by believing and speaking certain words. Romans 10:10 (NLT) says, "For it is by believing in your heart that you are made right with God, and it is by openly declaring your faith that you are saved."

Prayer of Salvation

If you would like to be saved and become a child of God, kindly say the prayer below.

> Dear Heavenly Father, I believe in Jesus Christ. I believe that he died for my sins and was raised from the dead. I declare that Jesus Christ is Lord of my life. I declare that I am saved in Jesus's name. Amen.

If you just said this prayer with faith, you are saved. Please continue to believe and live in his Word.

The Power of God's Word

God's Word can change any situation. With God all things are possible (Matthew 19:26).

God's Word has creative power (John 1:1–3).

God's Word will surely accomplish what it talks about in people's life (Isaiah 55:11).

God's Word is the source of miracles (Psalm 107:20).

God's Word brings healing and health to our bodies (Proverbs 4:20; Psalm 107:20).

God's Word brings good, success, and prosperity (Joshua 1:8).

Benefits of Faith Declaration

You can experience satisfaction in life by your words. Proverbs 18:20 (Berean Study Bible, BSB) says, "From the fruit of his mouth a man's belly is filled; with the harvest from his lips he is satisfied."

Speaking the right words brings good things, and hard work leads to compensation. Proverbs 12:14 (BSB) says, "By fruitful speech a man will be filled with good things, and the work of a man's hands will reward him."

Speaking the Word of God and reciting it produces good success and prosperity (Joshua 1:8).

Your words produce results for you. Proverbs 18:21 (International Standard Version, ISV) says, "The power of the tongue is life and death—those who love to talk will eat what it produces."

You can get justice and be set free by your words. Matthew 12:37 (BSB) says, "For by your words you will be acquitted, and by your words you will be condemned."

The right words can lead you out of trouble; you can be trapped by the wrong words. Proverbs 12:13 (BSB) says, "An evil man is trapped by his rebellious speech, but a righteous man escapes from trouble."

Your words can produce good things for you. Proverbs 13:2 (BSB) says, "From the fruit of his lips a man will enjoy good things, but the desire of the faithless is violence." As we speak God's Word, our situations change for good. Joel 3:10 (NIV) says, "Let the weak say, 'I am strong!'"

HOW TO USE THIS POTENT BOOK

Each chapter gives us declarations from God's Word concerning his will for us in that area of life. You can choose to declare God's Word for an area in which you want to see the power of his Word manifest in your life. You can also use the last chapter, which is a combination of faith declarations from different chapters, to provide declarations for every day of the week. For example, on Monday, you can use the Monday faith declarations and add any other chapter where you need a change.

How often should we speak the Word over our lives? Daily. We are encouraged to speak the Word daily. In Joshua 1:8 (GWT), God himself tells Joshua,

> Never stop reciting these teachings. You must think about them *night* and *day* so that you will faithfully do everything written in them. Then you will make your way prosperous and have good success.

This book is highly scriptural, and all the faith declarations are based on God's words in the Bible. The Bible counsels us to *speak things into being.* By declaring the words of God over our lives, we are speaking things the way they really are in the mind of God. We are declaring God's truth that brings us into oneness with what we speak. First Corinthians 1:30 (Good News Translation, GNT) says,

> But God has brought you into union with Christ Jesus, and God has made Christ to be our wisdom. By him we are put right with God; we become God's holy people and are set free. So then, as the scripture says, "Whoever wants to boast must boast of what the Lord has done."

By declaring our faith, we are also declaring what the Lord has done in our lives.

As you declare the words in this book, you are also invited to study the scriptures from which the declarations are derived. Using the book this way will make you more versed in God's Word for your personal life. These scriptures and declarations will lead to transformation, miracles, encouragement, strength, and comfort as you focus on the power of God's Word for your life.

I encourage you in using this book to be ready spiritually, mentally, and physically to receive the miraculous power of God's transforming Word.

FAITH DECLARATIONS
FOR MY FAMILY

It is important to speak God's Word over your family. God's blessing is literally in his Word. Every time God blessed, he *spoke* words. Genesis 1:28 (NLT) says, "Then God blessed them and *said*, 'Be fruitful and multiply'" (emphasis added).

By speaking God's Word over your family daily, you will experience the manifestation of his blessings in your family.

I say a special prayer that you will experience God's blessings and healing in your family, in Jesus's name. Amen.

- ❖ My family is living together in unity in Jesus's name. Amen. (Derived from Psalm 133:1)
- ❖ My children are my heritage from the Lord. (Derived from Psalm 127:3–5)
- ❖ I love my spouse just as Christ loves the church and gave himself up for us. (Derived from Ephesians 5:25)
- ❖ Patience, kindness, humility, trust, self-control, and the love of God are working in my family. (Derived from 1 Corinthians 13:4–8)

❖ I live at peace with everyone in my family. (Derived from Romans 12:18)

❖ I declare that my house and I will serve the Lord in Jesus's name. Amen. (Derived from Acts 16:31–34)

❖ The peace of Christ rules in my family since, as members of one body, we were called to peace. (Derived from Colossians 3:15)

❖ The Lord watches over my family when we are out of one another's sight. (Derived from Genesis 31:49)

❖ God is our refuge and strength, our helper who is always found in times of trouble. (Derived from Psalm 46:1)

❖ The Lord saves my family from all troubles. (Derived from Psalm 34:18–19)

❖ The Lord comforts and strengthens my family. (Derived from Isaiah 66:13)

❖ I will not provoke my children to anger; I will encourage them in the way of the Lord. (Derived from Colossians 3:21)

❖ My friends love me at all times, and my family stands with me in times of adversity. (Derived from Proverbs 17:17)

❖ I honor my parents and love my neighbor as myself. (Derived from Matthew 19:19)

❖ My children and grandchildren are my crown; my parents are my pride. (Derived from Proverbs 17:6)

❖ God has joined my family together, and we will not be separated in Jesus's name. Amen. (Derived from Mark 10:9)

❖ I receive my God-given spouse; my desire to be married will be fulfilled because the expectation of the righteous shall not be cut off. (Derived from Proverbs 23:18)

❖ The Lord is increasing us. My children, my family, and I are flourishing in Jesus's name. Amen. (Derived from Psalms 115:14)

❖ It is well with me; it is well with my spouse, my children, my lineage. It is well with my family in Jesus's name. Amen. (Derived from 2 Kings 4:26)

❖ Surely goodness and mercy follow us all the days of our lives, and my family and I will dwell in the house of the Lord forever and ever. Amen. (Derived from Psalm 23:6)

FAITH DECLARATIONS
FOR PROTECTION

As believers in Jesus Christ, we have divine covering under God's protection. According to the Bible, God is our protector and protection.

By speaking these Scripture verses daily, you will literally experience the manifestation of God's divine protection with testimonies in Jesus's name. Amen.

- ❖ My God is faithful; he will not let me be tempted beyond what I can bear. But he provides a way out for me. (Derived from 1 Corinthians 10:13)
- ❖ My Lord is faithful; he strengthens me and protects me from the evil one. (Derived from 2 Thessalonians 3:3)
- ❖ I am strong and courageous. I will not be afraid or terrified, for the Lord my God goes with me; he will never leave me nor forsake me. (Derived from Deuteronomy 31:6)
- ❖ I do not fear, for the Lord my God is with me. He strengthens me and helps me; he upholds me with the right hand of his righteousness. (Derived from Isaiah 41:10)

❖ If I unknowingly eat or drink any deadly thing, it shall not hurt me. (Derived from Mark 16:18)

❖ I cannot be yoked because I am anointed, and the anointing destroys every yoke. (Derived from Isaiah 10:27)

❖ The wisdom of God protects me; his understanding guards me. (Derived from Proverbs 2:11)

❖ I love the wisdom and Word of God for it protects and watches over me. (Derived from Proverbs 4:6)

❖ I am glad and sing for joy because God is my refuge, and he spreads his protection over me. (Derived from Psalm 5:11)

❖ The Lord arises and protects me. He establishes me in safety because I yearn for him. (Derived from Psalm 12:5)

❖ The Lord answers me when in distress; the name of the God of Jacob protects me. (Derived from Psalm 20:1)

❖ I am the righteousness of God in Christ Jesus. Though I may face challenges, the Lord delivers me from all of them. (Derived from Psalm 34:19)

❖ My God is my refuge and strength, an ever-present help in trouble. (Derived from Psalm 46:1)

❖ Have mercy on me, my God, have mercy on me, for in you I take refuge. I will take refuge in the shadow of your wings until the disaster has passed. (Derived from Psalm 57:1)

❖ The Lord delivers me from my enemies, O God; you are my fortress against those who attack me. (Derived from Psalm 59:1)

❖ Though I walk in the midst of trouble, you preserve my life. You stretch out your hand against the anger of my foes; with your right hand you save me. (Derived from Psalm 138:7)

❖ Keep me safe, O Lord, from the hands of the wicked; protect me from the violent, who devise ways to trip my feet. (Derived from Psalm 140:4)

❖ Though I may be pressed on every side, I will not be crushed; perplexed, but not in despair; persecuted, but not abandoned or destroyed for the Lord my God is with me. (Derived from 2 Corinthians 4:8–9)

❖ My God is my rock, in whom I take refuge, my shield and the horn of my salvation. He is my stronghold and my refuge. (Derived from 2 Samuel 22:3-4)

❖ I dwell in the secret place of the Most High, and I abide under the shadow of the Almighty. (Derived from Psalm 91:1)

❖ The Lord is my refuge and my fortress: my God; in him I trust. (Derived from Psalm 91:2)

❖ Surely he has delivered me from the trap of the enemy and from the deadly plague. (Derived from Psalms 91:3)

❖ He covers me with his feathers, and under his wings I trust: His truth is my shield and buckler. (Derived from Psalms 91:4)

❖ I refuse to be afraid for the terror by night nor for the arrow that flies by day. (Derived from Psalm 91:5)

❖ I am not afraid for the plague or pandemic that stalks in darkness nor for the destruction that wastes at noonday. (Derived from Psalm 91:6)

❖ Though a thousand fall at my side, and ten thousand at my right hand, it shall not come near me or my family. (Derived from Psalm 91:7)

❖ With my eyes I will behold and see the reward of the wicked. (Derived from Psalm 91:8)

❖ Because the Lord is my refuge and my habitation, no evil shall befall me, neither shall any plague come near my home. (Derived from Psalm 91:9-10)

❖ He has given his angels charge over me, to keep me in all my ways. (Derived from Psalm 91:11)

❖ His angels bear me up in their hands, to protect me from dashing my feet against a stone. (Derived from Psalm 91:12)

- ❖ I trample on the enemy; the devil is under my feet. (Derived from Psalm 91:13)
- ❖ The Lord has delivered me and has set me on high because of his name. (Derived from Psalm 91:14)
- ❖ I call upon the Lord and he answers me: he is with me in times of trouble; he has delivered me and will honor me. (Derived from Psalm 91:15)
- ❖ The Lord is my light and my salvation; whom shall I fear? The Lord is the stronghold of my life; whom shall I be afraid of? (Derived from Psalm 27:1)
- ❖ When evil men advance against me to devour my flesh, when enemies and foes attack me, they will stumble and fall. (Derived from Psalm 27:2)
- ❖ Though an army surrounds me, my heart will not fear; though war break out against me, even then will I be confident. (Derived from Psalm 27:3)
- ❖ I am still confident of this: I will see the goodness of the Lord in the land of the living. (Derived from Psalm 27:13)
- ❖ For in the day of trouble he will keep me safe in his dwelling; he will hide me in the shelter of his tabernacle and set me high upon a rock. (Derived from Psalm 27:5)
- ❖ Then my head will be exalted above the enemies who surround me; at his tabernacle will I sacrifice with shouts of joy; I will sing and make music to the Lord. (Derived from Psalm 27:6)
- ❖ With long life he will satisfy me and show me his salvation. (Derived from Psalm 91:16)

Chapter 5

FAITH DECLARATIONS FOR HEALING AND HEALTH

The Word of God is life and healing (medicine) to your whole body.

Proverbs 4:20–22 (NLT) reads, "My child, pay attention to what I say. Listen carefully *to my words.* Don't lose sight of them. Let them penetrate deep into your heart, for they bring *life* to those who find them, *and healing to their whole body*" (emphasis added).

God's Word carries his healing power. The Bible says that "*he sent his word and healed them,* and delivered them from their destructions" (Psalm 107:20 KJV).

By speaking God's Word to yourself daily, you will experience the healing power of God through his Word. God's Word is *spiritual medicine* without the possibility of overdose. My prescription to you is to take this *medicine* (faith declaration for health) morning, afternoon, and evening for divine healing and health.

I say a special prayer for you that you will experience health and healing through God's Word in Jesus's name. Amen.

❖ As I speak God's Word today, it brings healing to my body and health to all my flesh. (Derived from Proverbs 12:18, Proverbs 4:22)

❖ He sent his Word and healed me and delivered me from destruction. (Derived from Psalm 107:20)

❖ My Lord Jesus was wounded for my transgressions; he was crushed for my sins. The punishment that brought me peace was placed on him, and by his stripes I am healed. (Derived from Isaiah 53:5)

❖ The Spirit of God, who raised Jesus from the dead, lives in me. (Derived from Romans 8:11)

❖ And just as he raised Christ Jesus from the dead, he gives life to my body. (Derived from Romans 8:11)

❖ The Spirit of God gives life to my heart and blood vessels; by his stripes my heart and blood vessels are healed. (Derived from Romans 8:11, Isaiah 53:5)

❖ The Spirit of God gives life to my kidneys; by his stripes my kidneys are healed. (Derived from Romans 8:11, Isaiah 53:5)

❖ The Spirit of God gives life to my liver; by his stripes my liver is healed (Derived from Romans 8:11, Isaiah 53:5)

❖ The Spirit of God gives life to my pancreas; by his stripes my pancreas is healed. (Derived from Romans 8:11, Isaiah 53:5)

❖ The Spirit of God gives life to my muscles, bones, and joints; by his stripes my muscles, bones, and joints are healed. (Derived from Romans 8:11, Isaiah 53:5)

❖ The Spirit of God gives life to my blood; by his stripes my blood is healed. (Derived from Romans 8:11, Isaiah 53:5)

❖ The Spirit of God gives life to my head and brain; by his stripes my head and brain are healed. (Derived from Romans 8:11, Isaiah 53:5)

❖ The Spirit of God gives life to my mind; by his stripes my mind is healed. (Derived from Romans 8:11, Isaiah 53:5)

❖ The Spirit of God gives life to my reproductive system; by his stripes my reproductive system is healed. (Derived from Romans 8:11, Isaiah 53:5)

❖ The Spirit of God gives life to my intestines; by his stripes my intestines are healed. (Derived from Romans 8:11, Isaiah 53:5)

❖ The Spirit of God gives life to my eyes; by his stripes my eyes are healed. (Derived from Romans 8:11, Isaiah 53:5)

❖ The Spirit of God gives life to my nostrils; by his stripes my nostrils are healed. (Derived from Romans 8:11, Isaiah 53:5)

❖ The Spirit of God gives life to my skin; by his stripes my skin is healed. (Derived from Romans 8:11, Isaiah 53:5)

❖ The Spirit of God gives life to my digestive system; by his stripes my digestive system is healed. (Derived from Romans 8:11, Isaiah 53:5)

❖ The Spirit of God gives life to my lungs and respiratory system; by his stripes my lungs and respiratory system are healed. (Derived from Romans 8:11, Isaiah 53:5)

❖ The Spirit of God gives life to my nervous system; by his stripes my nervous system is healed. (Derived from Romans 8:11, Isaiah 53:5)

❖ The Spirit of God gives life to my immune system; by his stripes my immune system is healed. (Derived from Romans 8:11, Isaiah 53:5)

❖ The Spirit of God gives life to my lymphatic system; by his stripes my lymphatic system is healed. (Derived from Romans 8:11, Isaiah 53:5)

❖ The Spirit of God gives life to my excretory system; by his stripes my excretory system is healed. (Derived from Romans 8:11, Isaiah 53:5)

❖ The Spirit of God gives life to my endocrine system; by his stripes my endocrine system is healed. (Derived from Romans 8:11, Isaiah 53:5)

❖ The Spirit of God gives life to my exocrine glands; by his stripes my exocrine glands are healed. (Derived from Romans 8:11, Isaiah 53:5)

❖ Heal me, O Lord, and I will be healed; save me and I will be saved, for you are the one I praise. (Derived from Jeremiah 17:14)

❖ My faith in the name of my Lord Jesus makes me well; the Lord is raising me up in health and I receive forgiveness for my sins. (Derived from James 5:14–15)

❖ I worship you, O Lord my God, for you take away sickness. (Derived from Exodus 23:25)

❖ I will not fear, for the Lord is with me. He strengthens me and upholds me with his righteous right hand. (Derived from Isaiah 41:10)

❖ Jesus took my pain and bore my suffering. He was pierced for my transgressions and crushed for my iniquities; the punishment for my peace was on him, and by his stripes I am healed. (Derived from Isaiah 53:5)

❖ Jesus restores me to health and heals my body. (Derived from Jeremiah 30:17)

❖ Restore me to health, O Lord, and let me live. In your love you kept me from the pit of destruction; you have put all my sins behind your back. (Derived from Isaiah 38:16–17)

❖ You bring health and healing to me; you've blessed me with abundant peace and security. (Derived from Jeremiah 33:6)

❖ I declare that I prosper and live in health even as my soul prospers. (Derived from 3 John 1:2)

❖ I declare that the Word of God produces health in my whole body. (Derived from Proverbs 4:20–22)

❖ My cheerful heart is good medicine, but a crushed spirit dries up the bones. (Derived from Proverbs 17:22)

❖ There is a time for everything; this is my season and time for my healing (Derived from Ecclesiastes 3:1–3)

❖ I am dead to sin, and I live for righteousness. By Jesus's wounds I have been healed. (Derived from 1 Peter 2:24)

❖ I praise you, Lord. My soul will not forget all your benefits, for you forgave me and healed me. (Derived from Psalm 103:2)

❖ As Jesus healed every disease and sickness among the people, I trust him to heal my body today because Jesus is the same yesterday, today, and forever. (Derived from Matthew 4:23–24, Hebrews 13:8)

Chapter 6

FAITH DECLARATIONS FOR THE NEWNESS OF LIFE IN CHRIST

Speaking the faith declarations in this chapter will help you walk in the newness of life and keep your new life in Christ renewed and refreshed daily.

The Bible tells us about the renewing of the inward person (spirit) day by day (derived from 2 Corinthians 4:16).

We are also encouraged to walk in the newness of life in Romans 6:4 (BSB): "Therefore we were buried with him through baptism into death, so that, just as Christ was raised up out from the dead by the glory of the Father, so we also should walk in newness of life."

❖ I am a new creation recreated in true righteousness and holiness. (Derived from 2 Corinthians 5:17)
❖ I am born again. (Derived from John 3:3, 4, 7)
❖ I am born of the Spirit. (Derived from John 3:5–8)
❖ I confess that Jesus is the Lord my life. (Derived from Romans 10:9, Philippians 2:11)
❖ I walk in the newness of life just like Christ was raised from the dead. (Derived from Romans 6:4)

❖ I am saved by grace. (Derived from Ephesians 2:8)

❖ I am born of God because I believe that Jesus is the Christ. (Derived from 1 John 5:1)

❖ I know that I have passed from death to life. (Derived from 1 John 3:14)

❖ Old things are passed away, and all things are new in my life. (Derived from 2 Corinthians 5:17)

❖ I am the righteousness of God in Christ Jesus, sin has no power over me. (Derived from 2 Corinthians 5:21)

❖ I am washed, I am sanctified, and I am justified in the name of my Lord Jesus Christ and by the power of the Holy Spirit. (Derived from 1 Corinthians 6:11)

❖ I have dominion over sin by the grace of my Lord Jesus Christ. (Derived from Romans 6:14)

❖ I walk in righteousness and true holiness in the likeness of my God. (Derived from Ephesians 4:24)

❖ I am chosen by God, holy and beloved. (Derived from Colossians 3:12)

❖ I am chosen of God; therefore, I put on a heart of compassion, kindness, humility, gentleness, and patience, bearing with others and walking in forgiveness. (Derived from Colossians 3:12)

❖ I am chosen of God; therefore, I put on love, which is the perfect bond of unity. (Derived from Colossians 3:14)

❖ My old self was crucified with Christ, and I am no longer a slave to sin. I am the righteousness of God in Christ Jesus. (Derived from Romans 6:6)

❖ I am a new person, and I am being renewed to true knowledge according to the image of God, my father. (Derived from Colossians 3:10)

❖ I have put on the Lord Jesus Christ, and I make no provision for the flesh in regard to its lusts. (Derived from Romans 13:14)

- ❖ I am the temple of the Holy Spirit. (Derived from 1 Corinthians 3:16)
- ❖ As I look into the mirror of God, which is his Word, I am being transformed into his image that I see in the mirror from glory to glory, by the power of the Holy Spirit. (Derived from 2 Corinthians 3:18)
- ❖ I am a citizen of heaven. (Derived from Ephesians 2:19)
- ❖ I am clean by the Word of God. (Derived from John 15:3)
- ❖ Lord, please take away everything that causes me not to produce fruits. (Derived from John 15:2)
- ❖ Lord, thank you for pruning me so that I may be fruitful and productive. (Derived from John 15:2)
- ❖ I am born of God, and I have overcome the world. (Derived from 1 John 5:4)
- ❖ I am a true worshipper; I worship the Father in spirit and in truth. (Derived from John 4:24)
- ❖ My faith is the victory that has overcome the world. (Derived from 1 John 5:4)
- ❖ My inner person is being renewed day by day. (Derived from 2 Corinthians 4:16)
- ❖ I am dead to sin but alive to God in Christ Jesus. Amen. (Derived from Romans 6:11)
- ❖ I refuse to be in the practice of sin; I reject every habit of sin because I am born of God. (Derived from 1 John 3:9)
- ❖ Thank you, Lord, for taking away the heart of stone and giving me a new spirit. (Derived from Ezekiel 11:19)
- ❖ Through the riches of God's glory, I am strengthened with power through his Spirit in my inner person. (Derived from Ephesians 3:16)
- ❖ I am strengthened with all power, according to his glorious might in Jesus's name. Amen. (Derived from Colossians 1:11)

FAITH DECLARATIONS
FOR WALKING IN LOVE

The most important thing in Christianity is to love the Lord and to love our neighbors (derived from Mark 12:30–31). The Bible says that love is the greatest (derived from 1 Corinthians 13:13). Speaking God's Word over our lives helps us experience the manifestation of God's love and affects those around us as well. It also reminds us that we are called to love. It keeps us in the love of God.

> ❖ I walk in love that is patient, is kind, does not envy, does not boast, is not proud, does not dishonor others, is not self-seeking, is not easily angered, and keeps no record of wrongs. (Derived from 1 Corinthians 13:4–5)
> ❖ I do everything in love. (Derived from 1 Corinthians 16:14)
> ❖ I put on love, which is the perfect bond of unity. (Derived from Colossians 3:14)
> ❖ I declare that love and faithfulness will never leave me. I bind them around my neck; I write them on the tablet of my heart. I win favor and a good name in the sight of God and people. (Derived from Proverbs 3:3–4)

❖ I rely on the love God has for me. God is love. I live in love because I live in God, and God lives in me. (Derived from 1 John 4:16)

❖ I am completely humble, gentle, and patient, bearing with others in love. (Derived from Ephesians 4:2)

❖ I love because God first loved me. (Derived from 1 John 4:19)

❖ By the grace of God I walk in faith, hope, and love. But the greatest of these is love. (Derived from 1 Corinthians 13:13)

❖ Above all I love others deeply because love covers over a multitude of sins. (Derived from 1 Peter 4:8)

❖ My love is sincere, having no evil in it, and I cling to what is good. (Derived from Romans 12:9)

❖ I declare that Christ dwells in my heart by faith and I am rooted and established in love. (Derived from Ephesians 3:16–17)

❖ I love others as Christ has loved me. (Derived from John 15:12)

❖ I am devoted to others in love. I honor others above myself. (Derived from Romans 12:10)

❖ Dear Lord, direct my heart into your love and Christ's perseverance. (Derived from 2 Thessalonians 3:5)

❖ I love my family as Christ loved the church and gave himself up for her. (Derived from Ephesians 5:25–26)

❖ God lives in me, so I love others and his love is made complete in me. (Derived from 1 John 4:12)

❖ My love for God is manifested in my love for others. (Derived from 1 John 4:20)

❖ Thank you, Jesus, for your great love for me, whereby you died on the cross for me to have eternal life and be saved. (Derived from John 15:13)

❖ God has prepared for me what no eye has seen, what no ear has heard, and what no human mind has conceived because he loves me and I love him. (Derived from 1 Corinthians 2:9)

❖ My outstanding and continuing debt is to love others, for through loving others I fulfill the law of God. (Derived from Romans 13:8)

❖ I am a child of God because of his great love that he lavished on me. (Derived from 1 John 3:1)

❖ I refuse to walk in fear; instead, I walk in love because perfect love drives out all fear. (Derived from 1 John 4:18)

❖ My heart is filled with love because the love of God is poured into my heart by the Holy Spirit. (Derived from Romans 5:5)

❖ God is causing me to increase and abound in love for all people. (Derived from 1 Thessalonians 3:12)

FAITH DECLARATIONS FOR SPIRITUAL GROWTH

The Bible teaches that God's Word is spiritual food (milk as in 1 Peter 2:2 and strong meat or solid food as in Hebrews 5:12). Spiritual food helps us grow spiritually.

> Jesus answered, "Scripture says, 'A person cannot live on bread alone but on every word that God speaks.'" (Matthew 4:4 GWT)

Speaking the words of God below daily will help us grow spiritually.

* Thank you, Lord Jesus, for granting me the spirit of wisdom for revelation that I may continue to grow in the knowledge of God. (Derived from Ephesians 1:17)
* God is increasing the fruits of my righteousness. (Derived from 2 Corinthians 9:10)
* I speak the truth in love, and I am growing up in all aspects into Christ. (Derived from Ephesians 4:15).

❖ I walk in a manner worthy of the Lord, to please him in all respects, bearing fruit in every good work, and I am increasing in the knowledge of God. (Derived from Colossians 1:10)

❖ God is causing me to increase and abound in love for all people. (Derived from 1 Thessalonians 3:12)

❖ I am pressing on and walking in full maturity in Christ. (Derived from Hebrews 6:1)

❖ I receive the Word of God daily, so that by it I continue to grow in Christ. (Derived from 1 Peter 2:2)

❖ I add to my faith moral excellence, knowledge, self-control, endurance, godliness, and love for everyone. (Derived from 2 Peter 1:5)

❖ I am growing in the grace and in the knowledge of my Lord and Savior Jesus Christ. To him be the glory, both now and forever. Amen. (Derived from 2 Peter 3:18)

❖ I am growing in stature and in favor both with the Lord and with people. (Derived from 1 Samuel 2:26)

❖ I am growing in faith and becoming stronger in spirit, increasing in wisdom; and in the grace of God. (Derived from Luke 2:40)

❖ Like my Lord Jesus, I am increasing in wisdom and stature and in favor with God and with people. (Derived from Luke 2:52)

❖ I am increasing in the service of preaching the gospel and in witnessing that Jesus is the Christ everywhere I go, in Jesus's name. Amen. (Derived from Acts 9:22)

❖ When I was a child, I talked like a child, I thought like a child, I reasoned like a child. Now being in Christ, I put the ways of childhood behind me. (Derived from 1 Corinthians 13:11)

❖ I am confident that he who has begun a good work in me will complete it until the day of Jesus Christ. (Derived from Philippians 1:6)

❖ It is God who is at work in me, to will and to work in order to fulfill his good purpose. (Derived from Philippians 2:13)

❖ I walk in the fruit of the Spirit; I walk in love, joy, peace, patience, kindness, goodness, faith, gentleness, and self-control in Jesus's name. Amen. (Derived from Galatians 5:22–24)

❖ I am moving forward and becoming stronger and stronger in Jesus's name. Amen. (Derived from Job 17:9)

❖ I count it all joy when I fall into trials, knowing that the testing of my faith produces patience and perfection. (Derived from James 1:2–4)

❖ I rejoice in trials, knowing that trials bring about endurance, proven character, and hope; and hope does not disappoint because the love of God has been poured out within my heart by the Holy Spirit. (Derived from Romans 5:3–5)

❖ I run with endurance the race marked out for me, fixing my eyes on Jesus, the author and perfecter of my faith. (Derived from Hebrews 12:1)

Chapter 9

FAITH DECLARATIONS FOR DELIVERANCE FROM HARMFUL HABITS

Some Christians may struggle with certain harmful habits. In their heart of hearts, true Christians honestly desire to give up such habits but may find walking away from them challenging. The solution to this is in Joshua 1:8 (NIV): "Keep this Book of the Law *always on your lips; meditate* on it day and night, *so that* you may be careful *to do* everything written in it. Then you will be prosperous and successful" (emphasis added).

Meditating on God's Word helps us adhere to the Word. If you have struggled to follow God's Word in any area of your life, take the words of God concerning that area of life and speak them over your life daily. You will experience the power and enablement of God's Word. You will also be able to walk away from any harmful habits and walk the path in which God ordained that you should walk, in Jesus's name, Amen. You will be able to do God's Word easily without any struggle.

❖ The blood of Jesus Christ cleanses me from all sin and unrighteousness. (Derived from 1 John 1:7)

❖ I fast to loose the chains and untie the cords of the yoke, to set me free and break every yoke. (Derived from Isaiah 58:6)

❖ I walk in the light as he is in the light. (Derived from 1 John 1:17)

❖ I return to the Lord with all my heart, with fasting and weeping and mourning. (Derived from Joel 2:12)

❖ I am dead to sin but alive to God in Christ Jesus, amen. (Derived from Romans 6:11).

❖ I discipline my body like an athlete, training it to do what it should. (Derived from 1 Corinthians 9:27)

❖ I refuse to allow sin to reign or be master over me; I refuse to obey its lusts in Jesus's name, amen. (Derived from Romans 6:12)

❖ I refuse to present myself as an instrument of unrighteousness to sin, but I present myself to God as being alive from the dead. (Derived from Romans 6:13)

❖ I have dominion over sin by the grace of my Lord Jesus Christ. (Derived from Romans 6:14)

❖ I put to death the deeds of the body by the help of the Holy Spirit, and I am alive to God. (Derived from Romans 8:13)

❖ I am the righteousness of God in Christ Jesus; sin has no power over me. (Derived from 2 Corinthians 5:21)

❖ The devil is under my feet; the God of peace has crushed Satan under my feet. (Derived from Romans 16:20).

❖ I submit myself to God, and I resist the devil and he flees from me. (Derived from James 4:7)

❖ I am renewed in the spirit of my mind, and I am recreated to be like God in true righteousness and holiness. (Derived from Ephesians 4:24)

❖ I walk in righteousness and true holiness. (Derived from Ephesians 4:24)

❖ I am the light of the world; there is no darkness in me. (Derived from Matthew 5:14, 1 John 1:5)

❖ I walk away easily from sinful habits by the power of God's Word and by the help of the Holy Spirit. (Derived from 2 Timothy 2:21–23)

❖ The anointing of God breaks every yoke of sinful habits in my life. (Derived from Isaiah 10:27)

❖ I enjoy the liberty of the children of God that is in Christ Jesus. (Derived from Romans 8:21, Galatians 2:4)

❖ I know the truth, and the truth makes me free. (Derived from John 8:32)

❖ I am sin free; sin cannot attach itself to me. (Derived from Romans 6:7)

❖ I am free to serve God. (Derived from 1 Peter 2:16)

❖ The law of the spirit of life in Christ has made me free from the law of sin and death. (Derived from Romans 8:2)

❖ I am perfect as my father in heaven is perfect. (Derived from Matthew 5:48)

❖ I am awake to righteousness, and I do not sin. (Derived from 1 Corinthians 15:34)

❖ My High Priest Jesus Christ was in all points tempted and yet without sin. I therefore come boldly to the throne of grace, and I obtain mercy for a life free of sin. (Derived from Hebrews 4:15–16)

❖ I am called to follow the example of my Lord Jesus Christ, who committed no sin. (Derived from 1 Peter 2:21–22)

❖ I arm myself with the mind of Christ, and I refuse to live in the flesh but for the will of God. (Derived from 1 Peter 4:1–2)

❖ I abide in Christ, and I do not sin. I practice righteousness, just as he is righteous. (Derived from I John 3:6–7)

- ❖ O Lord, direct my steps by your Word, and let no iniquity have dominion over me. (Derived from Psalm 119:133)
- ❖ I regain dominion over every harmful habit by the Word of God and by the help of the Holy Spirit. (Derived from Psalm 8:6)

Chapter 10

FAITH DECLARATIONS FOR PROSPERITY

The term *prosperity* means "doing well in life." The idea of prosperity is from God and not from humans. In many Bible verses, God uses the word *prosper*. All parents want their children to do well in every area of life, and God also wants his children to do well in every area of their lives. He wants you to do well spiritually in your soul, in serving him, in your family, in school, on your job, in every honest endeavor, and also in your finances. In 3 John1:2 (BSB), we read, "Beloved, I pray that you prosper concerning all things and to be in good health, just as your soul prospers."

God said to Joshua in Joshua 1:8 (NLT), "Study this Book of Instruction continually. Meditate on it day and night so you will be sure to obey everything written in it. For then will you *prosper and succeed* in all you do" (emphasis added).

Several Bible verses used to create the faith declarations below show that God delights in the prosperity of his children. I pray that as you meditate and speak the words below daily, you will experience God's good success and prosperity in Jesus's name. Amen.

❖ I seek first God's kingdom and his righteousness, and every other thing I require is given to me as well. (Derived from Matthew 6:33)

❖ I experience good success and prosperity as I meditate on God's Word. (Derived from Joshua 1:8)

❖ My Lord God gives me hidden treasures and riches stored in secret places. (Derived from Isaiah 45:3)

❖ I shout for joy because the Lord delights in my prosperity. (Derived from Psalm 35:27)

❖ The blessing of the Lord makes me rich and adds no sorrow to it. (Derived from Proverbs 10:22)

❖ The Lord is my shepherd; I have everything that I need. (Derived from Psalm 23:1)

❖ He makes me lie down in green pastures. (Derived from Psalm 23:2)

❖ He restores my soul and renews my strength. (Derived from Psalm 23:3)

❖ I thank you, Lord, for blessing me with all spiritual blessings in the heavenly places. (Derived from Ephesians 1:3)

❖ God has prepared for me what no eye has seen, what no ear has heard, and what no human mind has conceived because he loves me and I love him. (Derived from 1 Corinthians 2:9)

❖ I am blessed, and I am a blessing to my world. (Derived from Genesis 12:2)

❖ I have all things that I require for life and godliness. (Derived from 2 Peter 1:3)

❖ All things are mine. (Derived from 1 Corinthians 3:21)

❖ I spend my days in prosperity and my years in pleasantness. (Derived from Job 36:11)

❖ I am a cheerful giver, and God loves me. (Derived from 2 Corinthians 9:7)

❖ I am rich toward God. (Derived from Luke 12:21)

❖ I give to the Lord generously, and I receive generously. (Derived from 2 Corinthians 9:6)

❖ People are giving unto me good measure, pressed down, shaking together and running over. (Derived from Luke 6:38)

❖ I live in prosperity and in good health, even as my soul prospers. (Derived from 3 John 1:2)

❖ Whatever I lay my hands to do prospers in Jesus's name. Amen. (Derived from Psalms 1:3)

❖ I thank you, Lord, for blessing me with the power to get wealth. (Derived from Deuteronomy 8:18)

❖ The wealth of the seas and the riches of the nations are coming to me. (Derived from Isaiah 60:5)

❖ The wealth of the nations are mine. (Derived from Isaiah 61:6)

❖ As God blew quails into the camp of Israel, so is my life overflowing with supernatural abundance. (Derived from Numbers 11:31)

❖ As God provided daily manna for the children of Israel, so is my life overflowing with daily supernatural provision. (Derived from Exodus 16:35)

❖ Blessed be the Lord my God, who daily loads me with benefits. (Derived from Psalm 68:19)

❖ All my needs are supplied according to his riches in glory by Christ Jesus. (Derived from Philippians 4:19)

❖ In Christ, I am the seed of Abraham and an heir of God's blessings according to the promise. (Derived from Galatians 3:29)

❖ I honor the Lord with my wealth and with the first fruits of all my labors. My storehouse is filled to overflowing, and my storage is bursting and overflowing with new abundance. (Derived from Proverbs 3:9–10)

❖ My progress and advancement are evident as I meditate on God's Word. (Derived from 1 Timothy 4:15)

❖ God blesses me abundantly and generously provides all I need so that I always have everything I need and plenty left over to share with others. (Derived from 2 Corinthians 9:8)

❖ I am enriched in every way so that I can be generous on every occasion, producing thanksgiving to God. (Derived from 2 Corinthians 9:11)

❖ I am like a tree planted by streams of water. I am fruitful and productive, and my prosperity never withers, and whatever I do shall prosper as I meditate on God's Word. (Derived from Psalm 1:2–3)

❖ Thank you, Lord God, as you make me abundantly prosperous in every work of my hand, making me fruitful and productive in every area of my life and rejoicing over me in Jesus's name. (Derived from Deuteronomy 30:9)

❖ I am blessed by my God to be fruitful, multiply, replenish the earth, and subdue it. (Derived from Genesis 1:28)

❖ I bring all my tithe and offering that there may be food in God's house as he opens the floodgates of heaven and pours out to me so many blessings to overflowing. (Derived from Malachi 3:10)

❖ I am an heir of God. (Derived from Romans 8:17)

❖ I am a joint heir with Christ. (Derived from Romans 8:17)

❖ I am who God says I am and I have what God says I have. All things are mine. (Derived from 1 Corinthians 3:21)

❖ I am increasing in the knowledge of my rich and glorious inheritance in Christ. (Derived from Ephesians 1:18)

❖ I know the grace of my Lord Jesus Christ, though he was rich, yet for my sake he became poor so that through his poverty I am rich. (Derived from 2 Corinthians 8:9)

FAITH DECLARATIONS FOR VICTORY AND DOMINION

The Bible teaches that our faith is the victory that helps us overcome everything we may face and every endeavor we may be tasked with in life. Speaking the faith declarations below daily will literally produce victory in your life.

- ❖ My faith is the victory that overcomes the world. (Derived from 1 John 5:4)
- ❖ I am born of God; therefore, I have overcome the world. (Derived from 1 John 5:4)
- ❖ Thanks be to God who gives me the victory through my Lord Jesus Christ. (Derived from 1 Corinthians 15:57)
- ❖ The Lord my God goes with me to fight for me and to give me victory in all things. (Derived from Deuteronomy 20:4)
- ❖ God is faithful; he will not let me be tempted beyond what I can bear. But he will also provide a way out for my victory. (Derived from 1 Corinthians 10:13)
- ❖ Challenges are bread for me; I eat them up. (Derived from Numbers 14:9)

❖ I have peace because I know that Jesus overcame the world for me. (Derived from John 16:33)

❖ I put on the full armor of God, and I stand strong on God's Word in the midst of challenges. (Derived from Ephesians 6:13)

❖ The trial of my faith is producing patience and perfection in my life. (Derived from James 1:1–5)

❖ I am strong in the Lord and in the power of his might. (Derived from Ephesians 6:10)

❖ God is for me; nothing and nobody can stand against me successfully. (Derived from Romans 8:31)

❖ I refuse to be afraid for God has put my enemies in my hands and none of them will be able to withstand me. (Derived from Joshua 10:8)

❖ Though I go through this battle, my victory rests with the Lord. (Derived from Proverbs 21:31)

❖ I refuse to fear in this challenge for the battle is not mine but the Lord's. (Derived from 2 Chronicles 20:15)

❖ Lord, you have given me the shield of your salvation, and your right hand upholds me; and your gentleness makes me great. (Derived from Psalm 18:35)

❖ Thanks be to God, who always leads me in triumph in Christ, and manifests through me the sweet aroma of his knowledge everywhere I go. (Derived from 2 Corinthians 2:14)

❖ I put my trust in nothing else, but I trust you, Lord, for my victory. (Derived from Psalm 44:6–7, Psalm 146:3, Psalm 21:31)

❖ Shouts of joy and victory resound on my side; the strong arm of the Lord has given me triumph. (Derived from Psalm 118:15, 16)

❖ Greater is he that is in me than he that is in the world. (Derived from 1 John 4:4)

❖ As David defeated Goliath, so I defeat all adversaries and adversity that comes my way in Jesus's name. Amen. (Derived from 1 Samuel 17:41–52)

❖ All things are working together for my good because I love God and am called according to his purpose. (Derived from Romans 8:28)

❖ The Lord subdues nations before me and paralyzes kings on my behalf; he opens doors and gates before me. He goes before me to make rough places smooth and to shatter the doors of bronze and cut through the gates of iron. He gives me hidden treasures and secret riches. (Derived from Isaiah 45:1–3)

Chapter 12

FAITH DECLARATIONS FOR STRENGTH

God's Word gives strength to our spirits, minds, and bodies. As you declare the words below daily, strength will rise from your spirit, affecting your mind and body in Jesus's name. Amen.

- ❖ As I hope in the Lord, my strength is renewed. I will soar on wings like eagles; I will run and not grow weary; I will walk and not be faint. (Derived from Isaiah 40:31)
- ❖ God is the strength of my heart and my portion forever. (Derived from Psalm 73:26)
- ❖ I can do all this through him who gives me strength. (Derived from Philippians 4:13)
- ❖ The Lord gives me strength and increases his working power in me. (Derived from Isaiah 40:29)
- ❖ The Lord gives strength to the weary and increases power to those who are weak. (Derived from Isaiah 40:29)
- ❖ I delight in persecutions, in difficulties, and in challenges. For when I feel weak, then he makes me strong. (Derived from 2 Corinthians 12:10)

- My flesh and my heart may fail, but God is the strength of my heart and my portion forever. (Derived from Psalm 73:26)
- I will not fear, for the Lord is with me; I will not be dismayed, for the Lord is my God. He will strengthen me and help me and uphold me with the right hand of his righteousness. (Derived from Isaiah 41:10)
- God has given me the spirit of power, of love and self-discipline. (Derived from 2 Timothy 1:7)
- I love you, Lord, my strength. The Lord is my rock, my fortress, and my deliverer; my God is my rock, in whom I take refuge, my shield and the horn of my salvation, my stronghold. (Derived from Psalm 18:1–2)
- But the Lord is faithful, and he strengthens me and protects me from the evil one. (Derived from 2 Thessalonians 3:3)
- I am looking to the Lord and his strength and seeking his face always. (Derived from 1 Chronicles 16:11)
- I am on guard; I stand firm in the faith; I am courageous; I am strong in the Lord. (Derived from 1 Corinthians 16:13)
- I will sing of your strength, in the morning I will sing of your love, for you are my fortress, my refuge in times of trouble. (Derived from Psalm 59:16)
- The Sovereign Lord is my strength; he makes my feet as surefooted as a deer, able to tread upon the heights. (Derived from Habakkuk 3:19)
- I am strong in the Lord and in his mighty power. (Derived from Ephesians 6:10)
- The Lord is my strength and my shield; my heart trusts in him, and he helps me. My heart leaps for joy, and with my song I will praise him. (Derived from Psalm 28:7)
- Through God's power that is at work within me, he is doing for me exceedingly and abundantly more than what I can ask

or can ever imagine in Christ Jesus. Amen. (Derived from Ephesians 3:20–21)

❖ I love the Lord my God with all my heart and all my soul, with all my mind, and with all my strength. (Derived from Mark 12:30)

❖ My strength is not by my might nor by my power but by the Holy Spirit in Jesus's name. Amen. (Derived from Zechariah 4:6)

❖ The message of the cross is the power of God at work in me. (Derived from 1 Corinthians 1:18)

Chapter 13

FAITH DECLARATIONS
FOR PEACE

God has called us to a life of peace and rest in Christ. As you declare the words in this chapter, I pray that you will literally experience the manifestation of deeper levels of God's peace in your life in Jesus's name. Amen.

- In peace I will lie down and sleep, for you alone, Lord, make me dwell in safety. (Derived from Psalm 4:8)
- The Lord blesses me and keeps me, makes his face shine upon me and is gracious to me; the Lord's face is toward me and he gives me peace. (Derived from Numbers 6:24–26)
- There may be trouble in the world and around me, but in Christ I have peace. In Christ I have overcome the world. (Derived from John 16:33)
- I will not let my heart be troubled, and I will not be afraid because the Lord has given me his peace. (Derived from John 14:27)
- I will not be anxious about anything, but in every situation, by prayer and petition, with thanksgiving, I present my

requests to God. And the peace of God, which transcends all understanding, guards my heart and my mind in Christ Jesus. (Derived from Philippians 4:6–7)

❖ I am a peacemaker because I am a child of God. (Derived from Matthew 5:9)

❖ I refrain my tongue from speaking evil. I seek peace and pursue it. (Derived from 1 Peter 3:10–11)

❖ The Lord of peace himself gives me peace at all times and in every way. (Derived from 2 Thessalonians 3:16)

❖ You keep me in perfect peace because my mind trusts in your word. (Derived from Isaiah 26:3)

❖ The peace of Christ rules in my heart; being a member of his body I am called to peace. (Derived from Colossians 3:15)

❖ Mercy, peace, and love are mine in abundance. (Derived from Jude 1:2)

❖ I am a peacemaker; I sow in peace and reap a harvest of righteousness. (Derived from James 3:18)

❖ I seek peace and pursue it. (Derived from Psalm 34:14)

❖ I make every effort to live in peace with everyone and to be holy; without holiness no one will see the Lord. (Derived from Hebrews 12:14)

❖ I make every effort to keep the unity of the Spirit through the bond of peace. (Derived from Ephesians 4:3)

❖ I have the wisdom that comes from heaven, which is pure, then peace-loving, considerate, submissive, full of mercy and good fruit, impartial, and sincere. (Derived from James 3:17)

❖ I put the Word into practice. And the God of peace is with me in Jesus's name, Amen. (Derived from Philippians 4:9)

❖ I have great peace because I love your Word and nothing can make me stumble. (Derived from Psalm 119:165)

❖ I am still and know that the Lord is my God; I will be exalted among the nations; I will be exalted in the earth. (Derived from Psalm 46:10)

❖ My mind is not governed by the flesh to produce death, but my mind is governed by the Spirit producing life and peace. (Derived from Romans 8:6)

❖ My honor is to avoid strife and every fool who is quick to quarrel. (Derived from Proverbs 20:3)

❖ I keep myself disciplined, which may not seem so pleasant at the time, but later on it produces a harvest of righteousness and peace for me being trained by it. (Derived from Hebrews 12:11)

❖ My feet are beautiful because I bring good news, proclaiming peace, bringing good tidings, proclaiming salvation, saying our God reigns. (Derived from Isaiah 52:7)

❖ I came to you in my weariness and burden, and you have given me rest and in you I have found rest for my soul. (Derived from Matthew 11:28)

FAITH DECLARATIONS AGAINST ANXIETY AND FEAR

Though the circumstances of life may produce fear and anxiety, God's Word encourages us not to fear or be anxious. As you speak the words of God in this chapter, fear and anxiety will diminish and eventually turn into courage and strength through the transforming power of God's Word in Jesus's name. Amen.

- ❖ The Lord is my light and my salvation, so why should I be afraid? (Derived from Psalm 27:1)
- ❖ The Lord is my fortress, protecting me from danger, so why should I tremble? (Derived from Psalm 27:2)
- ❖ God has not given me the spirit of fear but of power and of love and of a sound mind. (Derived from 2 Timothy 1:7)
- ❖ I refuse to be anxious or worry about my life or my provision. I cannot add a single hour to my life by worrying; rather, I seek first the kingdom of God and everything is given to me by my Father in heaven. (Derived from Luke 12:22–31)
- ❖ I cast my cares on the Lord and he sustains me; he will never let me fall. (Derived from Psalm 55:22)

- ❖ I sought the Lord, and he answered me; he delivered me from all my fears. (Derived from Psalm 34:4)
- ❖ When I am afraid, I put my trust in you, oh Lord. (Derived from Psalm 56:3)
- ❖ When anxiety was great within me, your consolation brought joy to my soul. (Derived from Psalm 94:19)
- ❖ God is my refuge and strength, an ever-present help in trouble. (Derived from Psalm 46:1)
- ❖ The Lord is with me; I will not be afraid. The Lord is with me; he is my helper. (Derived from Psalm 118:6–7)
- ❖ Even though I walk through the darkest valley, I will fear no evil, for you are with me; your rod and your staff comfort me. (Derived from Psalm 23:4)
- ❖ I am strong and courageous. I will not be afraid or terrified, for the Lord my God goes with me; he will never leave me nor forsake me. (Derived from Deuteronomy 31:6)
- ❖ The Lord is with me; I will not be afraid of what people can do to me. The Lord is with me; he is my helper. (Derived from Psalm 118:6–7)
- ❖ I prayed to the Lord, and he answered me. He has freed me, and I am free from all kinds of fear. (Derived from Psalm 34:4)
- ❖ I will not fear, for the Lord is with me; he will strengthen me and help me and will uphold me with the right hand of his righteousness. (Derived from Isaiah 41:10)
- ❖ I will not be anxious about anything, but in every situation, by prayer and petition, with thanksgiving, I present my requests to God. And the peace of God, which transcends all understanding, guards my heart and my mind in Christ Jesus. (Derived from Philippians 4:6–7)
- ❖ The love of God is working in my heart by the Holy Spirit and drives out all fear. (Derived from 1 John 4:18)

❖ I will be strong and courageous and not be terrified or discouraged, for the Lord my God is with me wherever I go. (Derived from Joshua 1:9)

❖ I refuse to worry about tomorrow, for tomorrow will worry about itself. (Derived from Matthew 6:34)

❖ I leave all my anxieties with the Lord because I know he cares for me. (Derived from 1 Peter 5:7)

❖ I will not be afraid; the Lord my God himself will fight for me. (Derived from Deuteronomy 3:22)

❖ I will not be afraid; instead, I will believe in God's assurance. (Derived from Mark 5:36)

❖ The Lord my God is in my midst, a victorious warrior. He will exult over me with joy, he will be quiet in his love, and he will rejoice over me with shouts of joy. (Derived from Zephaniah 3:17)

❖ I will say of the Lord, "He is my refuge and my fortress, my God, in whom I trust. He will cover me with his feathers, and under his wings I find refuge; his faithfulness will be my shield. I will not fear the terror of night, nor the arrow that flies by day, nor the pestilence that stalks in the darkness, nor the plague that destroys at midday. A thousand may fall at my side, ten thousand at your right hand, but it will not come near me. He will command his angels to guard me in all my ways. He will rescue me and protect me. I will call upon him in time of trouble, and he will deliver me and honor me. (Derived from Psalm 91:1–16)

FAITH DECLARATIONS FOR MENTAL HEALTH

The Word of God helps to stabilize the mind. The Bible says that he keeps our minds in perfect peace when we are always thinking of his Word. I have seen mental health issues dissolve and disappear through a daily practice of meditation. Meditation in Christianity involves thinking and speaking God's Word to ourselves. As you speak the words in this chapter over your life daily, I pray that you will experience the manifestation as stability and peace of mind in Jesus's name. Amen.

- ❖ You keep me in perfect peace because my thoughts are now fixed on you and I trust in your Word. (Derived from Isaiah 26:3)
- ❖ God has not given me the spirit of fear but of power and of love and of a sound mind. (Derived from 2 Timothy 1:7)
- ❖ When anxiety was great within me, your consolation brought joy to my soul. (Derived from Psalm 94:19)
- ❖ My mind is not governed by the flesh to produce death, but my mind is governed by the Spirit producing life and peace. (Derived from Romans 8:6)

- ❖ In peace I will lie down and sleep, for you alone, Lord, make me dwell in safety. (Derived from Psalm 4:8)
- ❖ There may be trouble in the world and around me, but in Christ I have peace. In Christ I have overcome the world. (Derived from John 16:33)
- ❖ I will not let my heart be troubled and I will not be afraid because the Lord has given me his peace. (Derived from John 14:27)
- ❖ I will not be anxious about anything, but in every situation, by prayer and petition, with thanksgiving, I present my requests to God. And the peace of God, which transcends all understanding, guards my heart and my mind in Christ Jesus. (Derived from Philippians 4:6–7)
- ❖ The peace of Christ rules in my mind; being a member of his body I am called to peace. (Derived from Colossians 3:15)
- ❖ I put the Word into practice. And the God of peace is with me in Jesus's name. Amen. (Derived from Philippians 4:9)
- ❖ God is the strength of my heart and my mind and my portion forever. (Derived from Psalm 73:26)
- ❖ I have great peace because I love your Word, and nothing can make me stumble. (Derived from Psalm 119:165)
- ❖ I came to you in my weariness and burden, and you have given me rest; in you I have found rest for my soul. (Derived from Matthew 11:28)
- ❖ Heal me, O Lord, and I will be healed; save me and I will be saved, for you are the one I praise. (Derived from Jeremiah 17:14)
- ❖ My faith in the name of my Lord Jesus makes me well; the Lord is raising me up in health, and I receive forgiveness for my sins. (Derived from James 5:14–15)
- ❖ I worship you, O Lord my God, who takes away my sickness. (Derived from Exodus 23:25)

❖ I refuse to fear, for the Lord is with me. He strengthens me and upholds me with his righteous right hand. (Derived from Isaiah 41:10)

❖ He took my pain and bore my suffering. He was pierced for my transgressions, crushed for my iniquities; the punishment for my peace was on him, and by his stripes I am healed. (Derived from Isaiah 53:4–5)

❖ Jesus restores me to health and heals my mind and body. (Derived from Jeremiah 30:17)

❖ You bring health and healing to me; you've blessed me with abundant peace and security. (Derived from Jeremiah 33:6)

❖ I declare that the Word of God produces health in my mind and my whole body. (Derived from Proverbs 4:20–22)

❖ There is a time for everything; this is my season and time for my healing. (Derived from Ecclesiastes 3:1–3)

❖ As Jesus healed every disease and sickness among the people, I trust him to heal my body today. (Derived from Matthew 4:23–24)

❖ I have the mind of Christ. (Derived from 1 Corinthians 2:16)

Chapter 16

FAITH DECLARATIONS
AGAINST DEATH

Untimely death is not God's will for his children. We will all leave this world one day. Some people may sleep, but we shall not all sleep. In 1 Corinthians 15:51 (NKJV), we read, "Behold, I tell you a mystery: We shall not all sleep, but we shall all be changed."

The words of God in this chapter will keep us from untimely death as we fulfill all of God's plans and purposes for our lives in Jesus's name. Amen.

- ❖ I will not die but will live and declare the works of the Lord. (Derived from Psalm 118:17)
- ❖ For you, Lord, have delivered me from death, my eyes from tears, and my feet from stumbling, (Derived from Psalm 116:8)
- ❖ I will walk before the Lord in the land of the living. (Derived from Psalm 116:9)
- ❖ I know that I will live to see the Lord's goodness in this present life. (Derived from Psalm 27:13)

- For you, O Lord, have delivered me from death and my feet from stumbling, so that I may walk before you in your life-giving light. (Derived from Psalm 56:13)
- But as for me, God will redeem my life. He will snatch me from the power of the grave. (Derived from Psalm 49:15)
- With all my heart I will praise you, O Lord my God. I will give glory to your name forever, for your love for me is very great. You have rescued me from the depths of death. (Derived from Psalm 86:12–13)
- Our God is a God who saves; he is the Lord, who rescues us from death. (Derived from Psalm 68:20)
- He redeems me from death and crowns me with love and tender mercies. (Derived from Psalm 103:4)
- Thank you, Lord, for you sent your word and healed me, and your word has rescued my life from the door of death. (Derived from Psalm 107:20)
- God has rescued me from death. O death, where is your sting? O grave, where is your victory? Thanks be to God, who gives us victory through our Lord Jesus Christ. (Derived from 1 Corinthians 15:55, 57)

FAITH DECLARATIONS
FOR LONG LIFE

- ❖ Thank you, Lord, for with long life you will satisfy me. (Derived from Psalm 91:16)
- ❖ I shall walk in all the ways which the Lord my God has commanded me; it is well with me, and my days are prolonged. (Derived from Deuteronomy 5:33)
- ❖ I will obey the Word of the Lord. It is well with me, and I will live long in the earth to serve the Lord. (Derived from Ephesians 6:1–4)
- ❖ God's Word adds long life and peace to my days. (Derived from Proverbs 3:2)
- ❖ As I serve the Lord my God, he blesses my bread and my water and removes sickness from me. There shall be no form of barrenness in my life; he will fulfill the number of my days. (Derived from Exodus 23:25–26)
- ❖ I will see good days and long life as I speak and declare good and not evil. (Derived from 1 Peter 3:10)

❖ You have shown me the path of life; in your presence is fullness of joy; at your right hand are pleasures forevermore. (Derived from Psalm 16:11)

❖ The Lord renews my strength like the eagle as I wait on him. I will run and not grow weary; I will walk and not be faint. (Derived from Isaiah 40:31)

❖ Even to my old age and gray hairs you, O Lord, sustain me. You have made me, and you will carry me. (Derived from Isaiah 46:4)

❖ When I am old and gray, do not forsake me, my God, till I declare your power to the next generation, and your mighty acts to all who are to come. (Derived from Psalm 71:18)

❖ God will make me still bear fruit in my old age; he will keep me fresh and green. (Derived from Psalm 92:14)

❖ Surely goodness and mercy follow me all the days of my life, and I will dwell in the house of the Lord forever and ever. Amen. (Derived from Psalm 23:6)

FAITH DECLARATIONS FOR EXCELLENCE IN LIFE

God called us to lives of excellence, glory, and virtue. As we speak God's Word in this chapter daily, we will experience the excellence and glory of God manifested in every area of our lives in Jesus's name. Amen.

- ❖ God called me into his glory and excellence; therefore, I declare that I walk in excellence in everything that I do. (Derived from 2 Peter 1:3)
- ❖ God has made me excellent, and he delights in me. (Derived from Psalm 16:3)
- ❖ I add to my faith moral excellence in Jesus's name. Amen. (Derived from 2 Peter 1:5)
- ❖ I have an excellent spirit in Christ. (Derived from Daniel 5:12)
- ❖ The spirit of excellence is at work in me. (Derived from Daniel 5:12)
- ❖ I am chosen of God, I am royalty, I am holy, and I display the excellence and perfection of God who called me out of darkness into his marvelous light. (Derived from 1 Peter 2:9)

❖ I spend my time thinking on things that are true, pure, lovely, and excellent. (Derived from Philippians 4:8)

❖ I am distinguished by exceptional qualities because the Holy Spirit, the Spirit of excellence, lives in me. (Derived from Daniel 6:3)

❖ I have the treasure of God in me, which is the excellence of God that works in me. (Derived from 2 Corinthians 4:7)

❖ The gifts of God in me produce in me the excellence of God. (Derived from 1 Corinthians 12:31)

❖ I keep my behavior excellent among unbelievers so that they may, because of my good deeds as they observe them, glorify God. (Derived from 1 Peter 2:12)

❖ I approve things that are excellent in order to be sincere and blameless until the day of Christ. (Derived from Philippians 1:10)

❖ I praise the Lord in songs for he has done excellent things for me, and I will make this known throughout the earth. (Derived from Isaiah 12:5)

❖ O Lord, my God, how excellent is your name in all the earth. (Derived from Psalm 8:9)

❖ I said to the Lord, "You are my Lord; I have no good or excellence without you." (Derived from Psalm 16:2)

❖ I offer excellent things and sacrifices to my God. (Derived from Hebrews 11:4)

❖ I am filled with the Spirit of God in wisdom, in understanding, in knowledge, and in all kinds of craftsmanship in Jesus's name. Amen. (Derived from Exodus 31:3)

FAITH DECLARATIONS FOR ENEMIES

- ❖ I will show love to my enemies, bless those who curse me, do good to those who hate me, and pray for those who spitefully use me and persecute me. (Derived from Matthew 5:4, Luke 6:27–28)

- ❖ The Lord is my light and my salvation; whom shall I fear? The Lord is the stronghold of my life; of whom shall I be afraid? (Derived from Psalm 27:1)

- ❖ When evil men advance against me to eat my flesh, when my enemies and my foes attack me, they will stumble and fall. (Derived from Psalm 27:2)

- ❖ Though an army surrounds me, my heart will not fear; though wars break out against me, even then will I be confident. (Derived from Psalm 27:3)

- ❖ I am still confident of this: I will see the goodness of the Lord in the land of the living. (Derived from Psalm 27:13)

- ❖ For in the day of trouble h will keep me safe in his dwelling; he will hide me in the shelter of his tabernacle and set me high upon a rock. (Derived from Psalm 27:5)

- ❖ Then my head will be exalted above the enemies who surround me; at his tabernacle will I sacrifice with shouts of joy; I will sing and make music to the Lord. (Derived from Psalm 27:6)

- ❖ Oh Lord, my God, come to me and save me; rescue me from my enemies. (Derived from Psalm 69:18)

- ❖ In blessing he blesses me and in multiplying he multiplies my seed as the stars of heaven and as the sand upon the seashore; and I will possess the gate of my enemies. (Derived from Genesis 22:17)

- ❖ My God makes the curses and evil thoughts from my enemies turn to blessings for me. (Derived from Numbers 23:11)

- ❖ For the Lord my God goes with me, to fight for me against my enemies, to save me. (Derived from Deuteronomy 20:4)

- ❖ The Lord will grant that the enemies who rise up against me will be defeated before me. They come against me from one direction, but they will scatter in seven directions. (Derived from Deuteronomy 28:7)

- ❖ And blessed be the Most High God, which hath delivered my enemies into my hand. And I will give him all my tithes. (Derived from Genesis 14:20)

FAITH DECLARATIONS AGAINST DEMONIC OPPRESSION AND DEMONIC ATTACKS

- ❖ Jesus gave me authority in his name; I have authority over all the power of the devil. (Derived from Luke 10:19)
- ❖ I trample on serpents and scorpions and destroy all the power of the enemy, and nothing shall by any means hurt me in Jesus's name. Amen. (Derived from Luke 10:19)
- ❖ I trample upon lions and cobras; I crush fierce lions and serpents under my feet by the authority and power in the name of Jesus. Amen. (Derived from Psalm 91:13)
- ❖ The devil and his demons are under my feet; I crush them under my feet in Jesus's name. Amen. (Derived from Romans 16:20)
- ❖ I cannot be yoked because I am anointed and the anointing destroys every yoke. (Derived from Isaiah 10:27)
- ❖ I cast out devils in Jesus's name. Amen. (Derived from Mark 16:17)
- ❖ The devil and his demons are subject to me in Jesus's name. Amen. (Derived from Luke 10:17)

❖ The God of peace has crushed Satan under my feet in Jesus's name. Amen. (Derived from Romans 16:20)

❖ I submit myself to God and I resist the devil, and he flees from me. (Derived from James 4:7)

❖ Get behind me, Satan! You cannot be a stumbling block to me anymore, in Jesus's name. Amen. (Derived from Matthew 16:23)

❖ The Lord rebukes you, Satan! The Lord, who has chosen Jerusalem, rebukes you! (Derived from Zechariah 3:2)

❖ The devil roams around like a roaring lion looking for someone to devour, but I resist him in the name of Jesus and I stand firm in the faith. Amen. (Derived from 1 Peter 5:8–9)

❖ I bind the dragon, that ancient serpent, who is the devil, or Satan. I bind you in Jesus's name. Amen. (Derived from Revelation 20:20)

❖ God has given me the authority and the backing of heaven, and whatsoever I bind on earth is bound in heaven and whatever I loose on earth is loose in heaven in Jesus's name. Amen. (Derived from Matthew 16:19, Matthew 18:18)

❖ I put on the full armor of God so that I take my stand against the devil's schemes, against principalities, against the powers of this dark world, against the spiritual forces of evil, and against wicked spirits in the spiritual realm in Jesus's name. Amen. (Derived from Ephesians 6:11–12)

❖ Therefore I put on the full armor of God so that I stand without falling when the day of evil comes; I stand my ground, and after I have done everything, I remain standing on the Word. (Derived from Ephesians 6:13)

❖ I stand firm, then, with the belt of truth buckled around my waist, with the breastplate of righteousness in place, with my feet fitted with the readiness that comes from the gospel of peace, and with my shield of faith, with which I extinguish all the flaming arrows of the evil one. (Derived from Ephesians 6:14–16)

❖ I slice and defeat the devil and his demons with my sword of the Spirit, which is the Word of God that I now declare in Jesus's name. Amen. (Derived from Ephesians 6:17)

FAITH DECLARATIONS FOR MY CALLING AND MINISTRY

- The love of Christ is the passion that compels and motivates me to serve in ministry. (Derived from 2 Corinthians 5:14)
- I love the Lord my God, and I serve him with all my heart and all my soul. (Derived from Deuteronomy 11:13)
- I choose this day that I and my house will serve the Lord. (Derived from Joshua 24:15)
- I serve the Lord with reverence. (Derived from Psalm 2:11)
- Like Paul the apostle, I count all things as nothing that I may win Christ. (Derived from Philippians 3:8)
- Like Jesus, I make myself nothing by taking the nature of a servant, and I humble myself like Christ to serve the living God. (Derived from Philippians 2:7–8)
- I serve the Lord with gladness and come before him with joyful singing. (Derived from Psalm 100:2)
- I look forward to the day I will stand before the Lord and he will say to me, "Well done, good and faithful servant! You have been faithful with a few things; I will put you in charge

of many things. Come and share your master's happiness!"
(Derived from Matthew 25:21)

❖ I will let my light shine before others so that they may see
my good deeds and glorify my Father in heaven. (Derived
from Matthew 5:16)

❖ God will not forget my work and my love for him, as I serve
and continue to serve others in ministry. (Derived from
Hebrews 6:10)

❖ As I serve, I am not looking to my own interests but to the
interests of others. (Derived from Philippians 2:4)

❖ I serve God and people in humility and in love. (Derived
from Galatians 5:13)

❖ I offer my body as a living sacrifice, holy and pleasing to
God—this is my true and proper worship and reasonable
service. (Derived from Romans 12:1)

❖ I am a soul winner. (Derived from Proverbs 11:30)

❖ I am full of zeal and keep my spiritual fervor serving the
Lord. (Derived from Romans 12:11)

❖ I serve the Lord with wholehearted devotion and with a
willing mind, for the Lord searches my heart and knows my
desires and my thoughts. (Derived from 1 Chronicles 28:9)

❖ I will be strong and will not give up, for my work will be
rewarded. (Derived from 2 Chronicles 15:7)

❖ I revere the Lord and serve him faithfully with all my heart,
remembering that he has done great things for me. (Derived
from 1 Samuel 12:24)

❖ I seek first his kingdom and his righteousness, and all things
I need will be given to me as well. Therefore I refuse to worry
about tomorrow. (Derived from Matthew 6:33–34)

❖ I go into my world and preach the gospel to all. Whoever
believes and is baptized shall be saved. (Derived from Mark
16:15)

❖ I live a life worthy of the calling I have received. I am completely humble, gentle, patient, and bearing with others in love. I make every effort to keep the unity of the Spirit through the bond of peace. (Derived from Ephesians 4:1–6)

❖ I have the mind of Christ, having the same love, being one in spirit and of one mind. I do nothing out of selfish ambition or vain conceit. Rather, in humility I value others above myself, not looking to my own interests but to the interests of the others. (Derived from Philippians 2:2–4)

❖ Not that I have already arrived at my goal, but I press on to take hold of that for which Christ Jesus took hold for me. But one thing I do: Forgetting what is behind and straining toward what is ahead, I press on toward the goal to win the prize for which God has called me in Christ Jesus. (Derived from Philippians 3:12–14)

❖ He has saved me and called me to a holy life, not because of anything I have done but because of his own purpose and grace. (Derived from 2 Timothy 1:10)

❖ As I share in the heavenly calling, I fix my thoughts on Jesus, whom I acknowledge as my high priest. (Derived from Hebrews 3:1)

❖ I throw off everything that hinders and the sin that so easily entangles. And I run with perseverance the race marked out for me, fixing my eyes on Jesus, the pioneer and perfecter of my faith who, for the joy set before him, endured the cross and its shame and sat down at the right hand of the throne of God. (Derived from Hebrews 12:1–2)

❖ I am a chosen generation, a royal priesthood, a holy nation, God's special person called to show forth the praises of him who called me out of darkness into his wonderful light. (Derived from 1 Peter 2:9–10)

❖ I revere Christ as Lord and am prepared to give an answer to everyone who asks the reason for the hope that I have in Christ. I do this with gentleness and respect, keeping a clear conscience, so that those who speak maliciously against my good deeds in Christ may be ashamed of their slander. (Derived from 1 Peter 3:15–16)

❖ I use my gift to serve others as a faithful steward of God's grace; I serve with the strength God gives me, so that in all things God may be praised through Jesus Christ. To him be the glory and the power for ever and ever. Amen. (Derived from 1 Peter 4:10–11)

FAITH DECLARATIONS FOR GOOD DREAMS AND VISIONS

We tend to have questions and need answers for the dreams we have. Dreams can come from God as direction, instruction, warning, foresight, insight, or hindsight. Knowing how to direct our dreams in life is instrumental in attaining success in life. Good dreams must be established and sealed in our lives through confession so they can materialize and become reality. Failure to do this can lead to missed spiritual opportunities and missed manifestation of God's good plan for our lives. The Bible says in Job 22:28 (NKJV), "You will also declare a thing, and it will be established for you; so light will shine on your ways."

- ❖ I declare that the good dream or vision (insert details of dream here) will become reality in my life in the mighty name of Jesus. Amen. (Derived from Proverbs 18:21)
- ❖ I decree that my God-given dreams and visions shall be established in my life in Jesus's name. Amen. (Derived from Job 22:28)
- ❖ I write my vision and make it plain, and I run with it. (Derived from Habakkuk 2:2)

❖ For my vision awaits its appointed time; it will surely come to pass; it will not delay in Jesus's name. Amen. (Derived from Habakkuk 2:3)

❖ The good plans of God for my life to give me a future and a glorious hope are surely coming to pass in Jesus's name. Amen. (Derived from Jeremiah 29:11)

❖ Thank you, Lord, for the gifts you have endowed me with, both the ones I am aware of and the ones I am discovering. Your gifts are being fulfilled in my life in Jesus's name. Amen. (Derived from Romans 11:29)

❖ Thank you, Lord, for giving me knowledge and skill in all learning and wisdom, in understanding of visions and dreams. (Derived from Daniel 1:17)

❖ The Spirit of the Lord is poured out upon me, and I see visions and dream dreams from God. (Derived from Joel 2:28)

❖ There is a God in heaven who reveals mysteries. He is my God revealing dreams and every mysterious thing to me. (Derived from Daniel 2:28)

Chapter 23

FAITH DECLARATIONS AGAINST BAD OR EVIL DREAMS AND VISIONS

Dreams can bring confusion, fear, and anxiety. This is an area of life where people tend to have questions and need answers. Bad dreams can be inspired by the circumstances of life that we face. They could come from life events or be related to things we fear or are anxious about. Dreams can also be engineered by the enemy and his cohorts.

Knowing how to direct bad dreams is critical for success in life. Bad dreams must be forbidden and cancelled by our declaration so they don't materialize. Failure to do this can lead to preventable evil experiences in life.

Jesus said in Matthew 18:18 (NLT), "I tell you the truth, whatever you forbid on earth will be forbidden in heaven, and whatever you permit on earth will be permitted in heaven."

- ❖ I bind, forbid, and cancel that bad or evil dream (insert details of dream here) in the mighty name of Jesus. Amen. (Derived from Matthew 18:18)

❖ I decree that it will not come to pass; it will not be established in Jesus's mighty name. Amen. (Derived from Job 22:28)

❖ No weapon formed against me shall prosper in Jesus's name. Amen. (Derived from Isaiah 54:17)

❖ When evil men advance against me to eat my flesh, when my enemies and my foes attack me, they must stumble and fall. (Derived from Psalm 27:2)

❖ I am still confident of this: I will see the goodness of the Lord in the land of the living. (Derived from Psalm 27:13)

❖ My God makes the curses and evil thoughts from my enemies turn to blessings for me. (Derived from Numbers 23:11)

❖ For the Lord my God goes with me, to fight for me against my enemies and to save me. (Derived from Deuteronomy 20:4)

❖ The Lord will grant that the enemies who rise up against me will be defeated before me. If they come against me from one direction, they will scatter in seven directions. (Derived from Deuteronomy 28:7)

❖ I trample on serpents and scorpions and destroy all the power of the enemy, and nothing shall by any means hurt me in Jesus's name. Amen. (Derived from Luke 10:19)

❖ I trample upon lions and cobras; I crush fierce lions and serpents under my feet by the authority and power in the name of Jesus. Amen. (Derived from Psalm 91:13)

❖ The devil and his demons are under my feet; I crush them under my feet in Jesus's name. Amen. (Derived from Romans 16:20)

❖ I cannot be yoked because I am anointed, and the yoke is destroyed because of the anointing. (Derived from Isaiah 10:27)

❖ The God of peace has crushed Satan under my feet in Jesus's name. Amen. (Derived from Romans 16:20)

✣ I submit myself to God and I resist the devil, and he flees from me. (Derived from James 4:7)

✣ Get behind me, Satan! You cannot be a stumbling block to me any more in Jesus's name. Amen. (Derived from Matthew 16:23)

✣ The Lord rebukes you, Satan! The Lord, who has chosen Jerusalem, rebukes you! (Derived from Zechariah 3:2)

✣ The devil roams around like a roaring lion looking for someone to devour, but I resist him in the name of Jesus and I stand firm in the faith. Amen. (Derived from 1 Peter 5:8–9)

✣ God has given me the authority and backing of heaven, and whatsoever I bind on earth is bound in heaven and whatever I loose on earth is loose in heaven in Jesus's name. Amen. (Derived from Matthew 16:19, Matthew 18:18)

✣ I put on the full armor of God so that I take my stand against the devil's schemes, against principalities, against the powers of this dark world, against the spiritual forces of evil, and against wicked spirits in the spiritual realm in Jesus's name. Amen. (Derived from Ephesians 6:11–12)

✣ Therefore I put on the full armor of God, so that I stand without falling when the day of evil comes, I stand my ground, and after I have done everything, I remain standing on the Word. (Derived from Ephesians 6:13)

✣ I stand firm, then, with the belt of truth buckled around my waist, with the breastplate of righteousness in place, with my feet fitted with the readiness that comes from the gospel of peace, and with my shield of faith, with which I extinguish all the flaming arrows of the evil one in Jesus's name. Amen. (Derived from Ephesians 6:14–16)

✣ I slice and defeat the devil and his demons with my sword of the Spirit, which is the Word of God that I now declare in Jesus's name. Amen. (Derived from Ephesians 6:17)

Chapter 24

FAITH DECLARATIONS FOR FAVOR AND BLESSINGS

❖ I am blessed in the city and blessed in the country. (Derived from Deuteronomy 28:3)

❖ My children are blessed. (Deuteronomy 28:4)

❖ All the works of my hands are blessed and prosper. (Derived from Deuteronomy 28:4, Deuteronomy 15:10)

❖ My harvest is blessed. (Derived from Deuteronomy 28:5)

❖ I am blessed in my going out and in my coming in. (Derived from Deuteronomy 28:6)

❖ The Lord has blessed my storage and everything I put my hand to do. The Lord my God has blessed me in this land. (Derived from Deuteronomy 28:8)

❖ The Lord has blessed me with abundant prosperity. (Derived from Deuteronomy 28:11)

❖ The Lord has opened the heavens, the storehouse of his bounty, to bless all the work of my hands. (Derived from Deuteronomy 28:12)

❖ The Lord has made me the head and not the tail. I will always be at the top and never at the bottom. (Derived from Deuteronomy 28:13)

❖ I am blessed when I mourn, for I am comforted. (Derived from Matthew 5:4)

❖ I am blessed in meekness, and so I inherit the earth. (Derived from Matthew 5:5)

❖ I am blessed to hunger and thirst for righteousness, for I will be satisfied. (Derived from Matthew 5:6)

❖ I am blessed to be merciful, for I will be shown mercy. (Derived from Matthew 5:7)

❖ I am blessed to be pure in heart, for I will see God. (Derived from Matthew 5:8)

❖ I am blessed to be a peacemaker everywhere I go, for this is the mark of the children of God. (Derived from Matthew 5:9)

❖ I am blessed when I am persecuted because of righteousness, because my reward is the kingdom of heaven. (Derived from Matthew 5:10)

❖ I am blessed when people insult me and persecute me and falsely say all kinds of evil against me because of my faith in Christ Jesus. I rejoice and I am glad because my reward is great in heaven. (Derived from Matthew 5:11–12)

❖ I trust in the Lord and my confidence is in him for he has blessed me and made me like a tree planted by the water; my leaves are always green, and I have no worries in a year of drought for I am fruitful and productive in all seasons. (Derived from Jeremiah 17:7–8)

❖ The Lord blesses me and keeps me; he makes his face to shine on me, he is gracious to me; his face is turned toward me, and he gives me peace. (Derived from Numbers 6:24–26)

❖ My Lord God grants me the desire of my heart and makes all my plans succeed. (Derived from Psalm 20:4)

❖ I commit everything I do to the Lord, and he establishes my plans. (Derived from Proverbs 16:3)

❖ I know the plans you have for me, O Lord God, plans to prosper me and not to harm me, plans to give me hope and a blessed future. (Derived from Jeremiah 29:11)

❖ My God supplies all my needs according to the riches of his glory in Christ Jesus. (Derived from Philippians 4:19)

❖ I worship the Lord my God; he has blessed my food and water. He has taken away sickness from me and my family. (Derived from Exodus 23:25)

❖ I have tasted and seen that the Lord is good; I am blessed because I take refuge in him. (Derived from Psalm 34:8)

❖ I love the Lord my God, and I walk in obedience to him; therefore, I live and increase, and the Lord my God has blessed me in this land. (Derived from Deuteronomy 30:16)

❖ I am blessed, I succeed, and I prosper because I trust in the Lord and heed his instructions. (Derived from Proverbs 16:20)

❖ Thank you, Lord, because you have blessed me openly for all to see. (Derived from Psalm 31:19)

❖ The grace of the Lord Jesus Christ is in my spirit. (Derived from Philemon 1:25)

❖ I do not repay evil with evil or insult with insult. On the contrary, I repay evil with blessing because I was called to inherit a blessing. (Derived from 1 Peter 3:9)

❖ I hunger and thirst for righteousness; therefore, I am blessed and satisfied. (Derived from Matthew 5:6)

❖ I bring my whole tithe into God's storehouse so that there may be food in his house; therefore, the Lord Almighty opens the floodgates of heaven and pours out so much blessing that my storehouse is overflowing with God's abundance. (Derived from Malachi 3:10)

❖ I am blessed because I have been called as a child of God, a peacemaker, reconciling people and also reconciling them unto God. (Derived from Matthew 5:9)

❖ Surely goodness and mercy follow me all the days of my life, and I will dwell in the house of the Lord forever and ever. Amen. (Derived from Psalm 23:6)

❖ I will seek God with all my heart and keep his word; his blessings are working in my life. (Derived from Psalm 119:2)

❖ The blessing of the Lord on my life brings wealth, without painful toil for it, in Jesus's name. Amen. (Derived from Proverbs 10:22)

❖ All these blessings have come on my life and accompany me because I believe in Jesus Christ and follow his Word. (Derived from Deuteronomy 28:2)

FAITH DECLARATIONS FOR
EVERY DAY OF THE WEEK

Monday Faith Declarations

Dear Father, in the name of the Lord Jesus and by the power of the Holy Spirit,

- ❖ I declare that I am a partaker of the divine nature. (Derived from 2 Peter 1:4)
- ❖ Christ in me is my hope of glory. (Derived from Colossians 1:27)
- ❖ My week is blessed; I am blessed in my going out. (Derived from Deuteronomy 28:6)
- ❖ I am blessed in my coming in throughout this week. (Derived from Deuteronomy 28:6)
- ❖ I am blessed in the city, and I am blessed in the field. (Derived from Deuteronomy 28:3)
- ❖ I am more than a conqueror in every endeavor or challenge in my life. (Derived from Romans 8:37)
- ❖ Greater is he that is in me than he that is in the world. (Derived from 1 John 4:4)

❖ As he is, so am I in this world. (Derived from 1 John 4:17)

❖ The same Spirit that raised Christ from the dead lives in me. (Derived from Romans 8:11)

❖ The Holy Spirit gives life to my body; therefore, I live in divine health. (Derived from Romans 8:11)

❖ The lines are falling unto me in pleasant places; I have a godly heritage. (Derived from Psalm 16:6)

❖ I do not conform to the standards of this world, but I walk in the perfect will of God. (Derived from Romans 12:2)

❖ I am the righteousness of God in Christ Jesus; sin has no power over me. (Derived from 2 Corinthians 5:21)

❖ I know that I have passed from death to life. (Derived from 1 John 3:14, John 5:24)

❖ I know that all things work together for my good. (Derived from Romans 8:28)

❖ I love God, and I am called according to his purpose. (Derived from Romans 8:28)

❖ My path is the path of the righteous. (Derived from Proverbs 4:18)

❖ My life is becoming brighter and brighter unto perfection. (Derived from Proverbs 4:18)

❖ I seek first God's kingdom and his righteousness, and every other thing I require is given to me as well. (Derived from Matthew 6:33)

❖ I experience good success and prosperity as I meditate on God's Word. (Derived from Joshua 1:8)

❖ My Lord God gives me hidden treasures and riches stored in secret places. (Derived from Isaiah 45:3)

❖ I shout for joy because the Lord delights in my prosperity. (Derived from Psalm 35:27)

❖ The blessing of the Lord makes me rich and adds no sorrow to it. (Derived from Proverbs 10:22)

- ❖ Whatever I lay my hands to do prospers in Jesus's name, Amen. (Derived from Psalm 1:3)
- ❖ I live in divine prosperity. (Derived from Proverbs 10:22)
- ❖ The Lord is my shepherd; I have everything that I need. (Derived from Psalm 23:1)
- ❖ He makes me lie down in green pastures; I have everything that I need. (Derived from Psalm 23:2)
- ❖ He restores my soul and renews my strength. (Derived from Psalm 23:3)
- ❖ People are giving unto me good measure, pressed down, shaken together, and running over. (Derived from Luke 6:38)
- ❖ I walk in love that is patient, kind, does not envy, does not boast, is not proud, does not dishonor others, is not self-seeking, is not easily angered, and keeps no record of wrongs. (Derived from 1 Corinthians 13:4–5)
- ❖ I do everything in love. (Derived from 1 Corinthians 16:14)
- ❖ I put on love, which is the perfect bond of unity. (Derived from Colossians 3:14)
- ❖ Above all I love others deeply because love covers over a multitude of sins. (Derived from 1 Peter 4:8)

Tuesday Faith Declarations

Dear Father, in the name of the Lord Jesus and by the power of the Holy Spirit,

- ❖ I declare that my Lord Jesus is the high priest of my confessions. (Derived from Hebrews 3:1)
- ❖ I have whatever I say. (Derived from Mark 11:23)
- ❖ I am born of God. (Derived from John 1:13)

- ❖ I have overcome the world because I am born of God. (Derived from 1 John 5:4)
- ❖ I live above this world. (Derived from Philippians 3:20)
- ❖ My affections are set on things above. (Derived from Colossians 3:2)
- ❖ Christ in me is my hope of glory. (Derived from Colossians 1:27)
- ❖ I know that I have eternal life. (Derived from 1 John 5:13)
- ❖ I live and function by the faith of the Son of God, Christ Jesus my Lord forever. (Derived from Galatians 3:20)
- ❖ Challenges are bread for me. (Derived from Numbers 14:9)
- ❖ I recreate my world by the Word of God. (Derived from Hebrews 11:3)
- ❖ Grace and peace are multiplying in my life and in my service to God. (Derived from 2 Peter 1:2)
- ❖ I have received the power of the Holy Spirit, and I am a witness of the gospel. (Derived from Acts 1:8)
- ❖ Though I walk through the valley of the shadow of death, I fear no evil, because my Lord is with me; his rod and staff comfort me. (Derived from Psalm 23:4)
- ❖ The Word of God makes me prosperous and gives me good success. (Derived from Joshua 1:8)
- ❖ I am a partaker of the divine nature. (Derived from 2 Peter 1:3–4)
- ❖ I am not a victim, but I am a victor in Christ Jesus. (Derived from 1 Corinthians 15:57)
- ❖ I am a king and a priest unto God. (Derived from Revelations 1:5–6)
- ❖ The Spirit of the Lord is upon me. He anoints me with power for service. (Derived from Luke 4:18)
- ❖ I am rich toward God, hallelujah! (Derived from Luke 12:20–21, 29)

❖ I declare that I prosper and live in health even as my soul prospers. (Derived from 3 John 1:2)

❖ I am blessed, and I am a blessing to my world. (Derived from Genesis 12:2)

❖ I have all things that I require for life and godliness. (Derived from 2 Peter 1:3)

❖ All things are mine. (Derived from 1 Corinthians 3:21)

❖ I spend my days in prosperity and my years in pleasantness. (Derived from Job 36:11)

❖ I am a cheerful giver and God loves me. (Derived from 2 Corinthians 9:7)

❖ I give to the Lord generously, and I receive generously. (Derived from 2 Corinthians 9:6)

❖ I declare that the Word of God is producing health in my whole body. (Derived from Proverbs 4:20–22)

❖ I declare that love and faithfulness will never leave me; I bind them around my neck, and I write them on the tablet of my heart. I win favor and a good name in the sight of God and man. (Derived from Proverbs 3:3–4)

❖ I rely on the love God has for me. God is love. I live in love because I live in God, and God lives in me. (Derived from 1 John 4:16)

❖ I am completely humble, gentle, and patient, bearing with others in love. (Derived from Ephesians 4:2)

❖ I love because God first loved me. (Derived from 1 John 4:19)

❖ By the grace of God I walk in faith, hope, and love. But the greatest of these is love. (Derived from 1 Corinthians 13:13)

Wednesday Faith Declarations

Dear Father, in the name of the Lord Jesus and by the power of the Holy Spirit,

- ❖ I declare that my life is moving from glory to glory. (Derived from 2 Corinthians 3:18)
- ❖ The blessing of the Lord makes me rich and adds no sorrow to it. (Derived from Proverbs 10:22)
- ❖ I am the light of the world. (Derived from John 8:12)
- ❖ I am from above. (Derived from John 15:19)
- ❖ I am the righteousness of God in Christ Jesus. (Derived from 2 Corinthians 5:21)
- ❖ I am an ambassador for Christ. (Derived from 2 Corinthians 5:20)
- ❖ I am a heavenly being on earth for God's mission. (Derived from Philippians 3:20)
- ❖ The love of God is shed abroad in my heart by the Holy Spirit. (Derived from Romans 5:5)
- ❖ My path is a shining light that shines brighter and brighter unto the perfect day. (Derived from Proverbs 4:18)
- ❖ My faith is the victory that overcomes the world. (Derived from 1 John 5:4–5)
- ❖ I'm looking unto Jesus the author and finisher of my faith. (Derived from Hebrews 12:2)
- ❖ No weapon formed against me shall prosper. (Derived from Isaiah 54:17)
- ❖ I fear no evil because my Lord is with me; his rod and staff comfort me. (Derived from Psalm 23:4)
- ❖ The Lord watches over my going out and coming in. (Derived from Psalm 121:8)

❖ No harm will come near me, no disaster will come near my home, and his angels guard me (Derived from Psalm 91:10–11)

❖ My faith in the name of my Lord Jesus makes me well; the Lord is raising me up in health, and I receive forgiveness for my sins. (Derived from James 5:14–15)

❖ I worship you, O Lord my God, who takes away my sickness. (Derived from Exodus 23:25)

❖ I refuse to fear, for the Lord is with me. He strengthens me and upholds me with his righteous right hand. (Derived from Isaiah 41:10)

❖ I live in prosperity and in good health, even as my soul prospers. (Derived from 3 John 1:2)

❖ Whatever I lay my hands to do prospers in Jesus's name, amen. (Derived from Psalm 1:3)

❖ I thank you, Lord, for blessing me with the power to get wealth. (Derived from Deuteronomy 8:18)

❖ The wealth of the seas and the riches of the nations are coming to me. (Derived from Isaiah 60:5)

❖ The riches of the Gentiles are mine. (Derived from Isaiah 61:6)

❖ As God blew quails into the camp of Israel so is my life overflowing with supernatural abundance. (Derived from Numbers 11:31)

❖ As God provided daily manna for the children of Israel, so is my life overflowing with daily supernatural provision. (Derived from Exodus 16:35)

❖ He took my pain and bore my suffering. He was pierced for my transgressions, crushed for my iniquities; the punishment for my peace was on him, and by his stripes I am healed. (Derived from Isaiah 53:5)

❖ I declare that Christ dwells in my heart by faith, and I am rooted and established in love. (Derived from Ephesians 3:16–17)

❖ I love others as Christ has loved me. (Derived from John 15:12)

❖ I am devoted to others in love. I honor others above myself. (Derived from Romans 12:10)

❖ Dear Lord, direct my heart into your love and Christ's perseverance. (Derived from 2 Thessalonians 3:5)

❖ I love my family as Christ loved the church and gave himself up for her. (Derived from Ephesians 5:25–26)

❖ God lives in me, so I love others and his love is made complete in me. (Derived from 1 John 4:12)

❖ My love for God is manifested in my love for others. (Derived from 1 John 4:20)

❖ Thank you, Jesus, for your great love for me, whereby you died on the cross for me to have eternal life and be saved. (Derived from John 15:13)

❖ Surely goodness and mercy follow me all the days of my life, and I will dwell in the house of the Lord forever and ever. Amen. (Derived from Psalm 23:6)

Thursday Faith Declarations

Dear Father, in the name of the Lord Jesus and by the power of the Holy Spirit,

❖ I declare that I walk in the Spirit. (Derived from Galatians 5:16)

❖ I walk in love. (Derived from Ephesians 5:2)

❖ I am full of God's Spirit. (Derived from John 14:16–17)

❖ I am complete in Christ. (Derived from Colossians 2:10)

❖ My sufficiency is of him. (Derived from 2 Corinthians 3:5)

❖ I am the seed of Abraham. (Derived from Galatians 3:29)

❖ I am a new creation in Christ. (Derived from 2 Corinthians 5:17)

❖ I am justified by faith, and I am at peace with God. (Derived from Romans 5:1)

❖ I am crucified with Christ; I do not live for myself but for Christ. (Derived from Galatians 2:20)

❖ The life I live now is by the faith of the Son of God. (Derived from Galatians 2:20)

❖ I am anxious for nothing but in everything by prayer and supplication I make my request known to God. (Derived from Philippians 4:6)

❖ I have peace that surpasses all understanding in my spirit, soul, and body. (Derived from Philippians 4:7)

❖ I live in God's rest. (Derived from Hebrews 4:9)

❖ I cast all my cares on Jesus because I know that he cares for me. (Derived from 1 Peter 5:7)

❖ I refuse to worry because I know that God loves me. (Derived from John 16:27)

❖ I have an excellent spirit. (Derived from Daniel 6:3)

❖ My body is the temple of the Holy Spirit. (Derived from 1 Corinthians 6:19–20)

❖ I have authority over all devils, in the name of Jesus. (Derived from Luke 9:1)

❖ Greater is he that is in me than he that is in the world. (Derived from 1 John 4:4)

❖ I am your battle-axe and your weapon of war. (Derived from Jeremiah 51:20)

❖ I am a king and priest unto my God. (Derived from Revelation 1:6)

- ❖ I am strong in the Lord and in the power of his might. (Derived from Ephesians 6:10)
- ❖ I have favor with God and with men. (Derived from Proverbs 3:4)
- ❖ I am a cheerful giver. (Derived from 2 Corinthians 9:7)
- ❖ Blessed be the Lord my God, who daily loads me with benefits. (Derived from Psalm 68:19)
- ❖ All my needs are supplied according to his riches in glory by Christ Jesus. (Derived from Philippians 4:19)
- ❖ In Christ, I am the seed of Abraham and an heir of God's blessings according to the promise. (Derived from Galatians 3:29)
- ❖ My Lord Jesus was wounded for my transgressions, and he was crushed for my sins; the punishment that brought me peace was placed on him, and by his stripes I am healed. (Derived from Isaiah 53:5)
- ❖ The Spirit of God, who raised Jesus from the dead, lives in me. (Derived from Romans 8:11)
- ❖ And just as he raised Christ Jesus from the dead, he gives life to my body. (Derived from Romans 8:11)
- ❖ My faith is the victory that has overcome the world (Derived from 1 John 5:4)
- ❖ My inner person is being renewed day by day (Derived from 2 Corinthians 4:16)
- ❖ I am dead to sin but alive to God in Christ Jesus, amen. (Derived from Romans 6:11)
- ❖ God has prepared for me what no eye has seen, what no ear has heard, and what no human mind has conceived because he loves me and I love him. (Derived from 1 Corinthians 2:9)
- ❖ My outstanding and continuing debt is to love others, for through loving others I fulfill the law of God. (Derived from Romans 13:8)

Friday Faith Declarations

Dear Father, in the name of the Lord Jesus and by the power of the Holy Spirit,

- ❖ I declare that the joy of the Lord is my strength. (Derived from Nehemiah 8:10)
- ❖ I am going about doing good, healing the sick, and preaching the gospel. (Derived from Matthew 10:7–8)
- ❖ I belong to God; my life is not my own. (Derived from 1 John 5:1)
- ❖ The Spirit of the Lord is upon me. (Derived from Luke 4:18–19)
- ❖ I am growing in grace and in the knowledge of God. (Derived from 2 Peter 3:18)
- ❖ I am God's handiwork, created in Christ Jesus unto good works. (Derived from Ephesians 2:10)
- ❖ I am crucified with Christ, nevertheless I live, yet not I but Christ. (Derived from Galatians 2:20)
- ❖ I am rooted and grounded in love. (Derived from Ephesians 3:17–19)
- ❖ Christ is the rock of my salvation and by his grace I will make the rapture. (Derived from Psalm 62:6)
- ❖ All things are possible to me. (Derived from Mark 10:27)
- ❖ I can do all things through Christ, who strengthens me. (Derived from Philippians 4:13)
- ❖ I refuse to be poor. Jesus became poor for me, and through his poverty, I am rich. (Derived from 2 Corinthians 8:9)
- ❖ I am seated with Christ in heavenly places far above principalities, power, the devil, demons, evil spirits, witchcraft, and voodoo. (Derived from Ephesians 2:6)
- ❖ I cast out devils in Jesus's name. (Derived from Mark 16:17)

- I am a new person, and I am being renewed in knowledge according to the image of Christ r. (Derived from Colossians 3:10)
- I have put on the Lord Jesus Christ, and I make no provision for the flesh in regard to its lusts. (Derived from Romans 13:14)
- I am the temple of the Holy Spirit. (Derived from 1 Corinthians 3:16)
- As I look into the mirror of God, which is his Word, I am being transformed into his image that I see in the mirror from glory to glory, by the Holy Spirit. (Derived from 2 Corinthians 3:18)
- I am a citizen of heaven. (Derived from Ephesians 2:19)
- I am clean by the Word of God. (Derived from John 15:3)
- Lord, please take away everything that causes me not to produce fruits. (Derived from John 15:2)
- Lord, thank you for pruning me that I may be fruitful and productive. (Derived from John 15:2)
- I honor the Lord with my wealth and with the first fruits of all my labors. My store house is filled to overflowing, and my storage is bursting and overflowing with new abundance. (Derived from Proverbs 3:9–10)
- God blesses me abundantly and generously provides all I need so that I always have everything I need and plenty left over to share with others. (Derived from 2 Corinthians 9:8)
- I am enriched in every way so that I can be generous on every occasion producing thanksgiving to God. (Derived from 2 Corinthians 9:11)
- I am born of God, and I have overcome the world. (Derived from 1 John 5:4)
- I refuse to be in the practice of sin. I reject every habit of sin because I am born of God. (Derived from 1 John 3:9)

❖ Through the riches of God's glory, I am strengthened with power through his Spirit in my inner person. (Derived from Ephesians 3:16)

❖ I am strengthened with all power, according to his glorious might. (Derived from Colossians 1:11)

❖ I am a true worshipper; I worship the Father in Spirit and in truth. (Derived from John 4:24)

❖ I am a child of God because of his great love that he lavished on me. (Derived from 1 John 3:1)

Saturday Faith Declarations

Dear Father, in the name of the Lord Jesus and by the power of the Holy Spirit,

❖ I declare that my life is full of joy unspeakable and full of glory. (Derived from 1 Peter 1:8)

❖ I live out my days in prosperity, and I spend my years in pleasantness. (Derived from Job 36:11)

❖ He causes me to triumph always. (Derived from 2 Corinthians 2:14)

❖ I am anointed to preach the gospel to the poor, to heal the brokenhearted, to preach deliverance to the captives, and recover sight to the blind. (Derived from Luke 4:18)

❖ Jesus is Lord of my life. (Derived from Romans 10:9, 1 Corinthians 8:6)

❖ I have the keys to the mysteries of the kingdom. (Derived from Matthew 16:19)

❖ Glorious things are spoken of me. (Derived from Psalm 87:3)

❖ I am the head and not the tail. (Derived from Deuteronomy 28:13)

❖ I am filled with all the fullness of God. (Derived from Ephesians 3:19)

❖ I have the Spirit of the fear of the Lord; therefore, I have reverent fear in all my dealing with God, God's people, and the things of God. (Derived from Isaiah 11:2-3)

❖ The Spirit of wisdom, knowledge, understanding, and counsel is at work in me. (Derived from Isaiah 11:2)

❖ The Lord is my defense. (Derived from Psalm 94:22)

❖ I have the Spirit of wisdom for revelation in the knowledge of God. (Ephesians 1:17)

❖ I have divine immunity. (Derived from Deuteronomy 7:15)

❖ I know that I have passed from death to life. (Derived from 1 John 3:14)

❖ I walk in the newness of life just like Christ was raised from the dead. (Derived from Romans 6:4)

❖ I am saved by grace. (Derived from Ephesians 2:8)

❖ I am born of God because I believe that Jesus is the Christ. (Derived from 1 John 5:1)

❖ Old things are passed away, and all things are new in my life (Derived from 2 Corinthians 5:17)

❖ My progress and advancement are evident as I meditate on God's Word. (Derived from 1 Timothy 4:15)

❖ I am like a tree planted by streams of water; I am fruitful and productive, and my prosperity never withers, and whatever I do shall prosper as I meditate on God's Word. (Derived from Psalm 1:2-3)

❖ Thank you, Lord God, as you make me abundantly prosperous in every work of my hand, making me fruitful and productive in every area of my life and rejoicing over me in Jesus's name. (Derived from Deuteronomy 30:9)

❖ I am blessed by my God to be fruitful, and multiply, and replenish the earth, and subdue it. (Derived from Genesis 1:28)

❖ I bring all my tithe and offering that there may be food in God's house as he opens the floodgates of heaven and pours out to me so many blessings to overflowing. (Derived from Malachi 3:10)

❖ I am the righteousness of God in Christ Jesus; sin has no power over me. (Derived from 2 Corinthians 5:21)

❖ I am washed, I am sanctified, and I am justified in the name of my Lord Jesus Christ and by the power of the Holy Spirit. (Derived from 1 Corinthians 6:11)

❖ I have dominion over sin by the grace of my Lord Jesus Christ. (Derived from Romans 6:14)

❖ I walk in righteousness and true holiness in the likeness of Christ. (Derived from Ephesians 4:24)

❖ I am chosen by God, holy and beloved. (Derived from Colossians 3:12)

❖ I am chosen of God; therefore, I put on a heart of compassion, kindness, humility, gentleness, patience, bearing with others, and forgiveness. (Derived from Colossians 3:12)

❖ I am chosen of God; therefore, I put on love, which is the perfect bond of unity. (Derived from Colossians 3:14)

❖ My old self was crucified with Christ, and I am no longer a slave to sin. I am the righteousness of God in Christ Jesus. (Derived from Romans 6:6)

❖ I refuse to walk in fear; instead, I walk in love because perfect love drives out all fear. (Derived from 1 John 4:18)

Sunday Faith Declarations

Dear Father, in the name of the Lord Jesus and by the power of the Holy Spirit,

- ❖ I declare that I am blessed with all spiritual blessings in the heavenly places. (Derived from Ephesians 1:3)
- ❖ I have all things that I require for life and godliness. (Derived from 2 Peter 1:3)
- ❖ His grace is sufficient for me. (Derived from 2 Corinthians 12:9)
- ❖ I walk in the light as he is in the light. (Derived from 1 John 1:7)
- ❖ I am not of this world; I am from above. (Derived from John 17:14)
- ❖ I am pressing toward the mark of my high calling in him. (Derived from Philippians 3:14)
- ❖ The law of the spirit of life has made me free from the law of sin and death. (Derived from Romans 8:2)
- ❖ I have the victory through Jesus Christ. (Derived from 1 Corinthians 15:57)
- ❖ I am an ambassador for Christ. (Derived from 2 Corinthians 5:20)
- ❖ God supplies all my needs according to his riches in glory by Christ Jesus. (Derived from Philippians 4:19)
- ❖ I declare that I am a new creation. (Derived from 2 Corinthians 5:17)
- ❖ I am the righteousness of God in Christ Jesus. (Derived from 2 Corinthians 5:21)
- ❖ I am more than a conqueror. (Derived from Romans 8:37)
- ❖ I have the mind of Christ. (Derived from 1 Corinthians 2:16)
- ❖ I am blessed, and I am a blessing to my world. (Derived from Genesis 12:2)

- ❖ I have all things that I require for life and godliness. (Derived from 2 Peter 1:3)
- ❖ I spend my days in prosperity and my years in pleasantness. (Derived from Job 36:11)
- ❖ I am strong in the Lord and in the power of his might. (Derived from Ephesians 6:10)
- ❖ The love of God has been poured out into my heart by the Holy Spirit. (Derived from Romans 5:5)
- ❖ God's love makes me filled with all the fullness of God in Christ Jesus. (Derived from Ephesians 3:19)
- ❖ I am complete in Christ Jesus. (Derived from Colossians 2:10)
- ❖ I arise and shine, for the glory of the Lord has risen upon me. (Derived from Isaiah 60:1)
- ❖ I am an heir of God. (Derived from Romans 8:17)
- ❖ I am a joint heir with Christ. (Derived from Romans 8:17)
- ❖ I am who God says I am, and I have what God says I have. All things are mine. (Derived from 1 Corinthians 3:21)
- ❖ I am increasing in the knowledge of my rich and glorious inheritance in Christ. (Derived from Ephesians 1:18)
- ❖ I know the grace of my Lord Jesus Christ; though he was rich, yet for my sake he became poor, so that through his poverty I am rich. (Derived from 2 Corinthians 8:9)
- ❖ Unbelievers are coming to my light, and kings are coming to the brightness of my rising. (Derived from Isaiah 60:3)
- ❖ I am not ashamed of the gospel of Christ for it is the power of God unto salvation. (Derived from Romans 1:16)
- ❖ The wisdom of God makes me a soul winner; I declare that I am winning souls into God's kingdom. (Derived from Proverbs 11:30)
- ❖ I walk in a manner worthy of the Lord, to please him in all respects, bearing fruit in every good work, and

I am increasing in the knowledge of God (Derived from Colossians 1:10)

❖ God is causing me to increase and abound in love for all people. (Derived from 1 Thessalonians 3:12)

❖ I am pressing on to full maturity in Christ. (Derived from Hebrews 6:1)

❖ I receive and speak the Word of God daily so that I may grow in Christ. (Derived from 1 Peter 2:2)

❖ I add to my faith moral excellence, knowledge, self-control, endurance, godliness, and love for everyone. (Derived from 2 Peter 1:5)

❖ My heart is filled with love because the love of God is poured into my heart by the Holy Spirit. (Derived from Romans 5:5)

ABOUT THE AUTHOR

Dr. Ken Ezimoha is a medical doctor and pastor who, through the leading of God's Word, has raised pastors and leaders around the United States for the kingdom of God. He and his lovely wife, Mary Ezimoha, are passionately involved in teaching the truth, spreading God's Word, and building lives in Christ.

Printed in the United States
by Baker & Taylor Publisher Services